D0095093

SOLFERINO

The Birth of a Nation

By the same author:

Napoleon's Second Empress
Dunkirk: Anatomy of Disaster
Dordogne

SOLFERINO

The Birth of a Nation

Lt.-Col. PATRICK TURNBULL

St. Martin's Press
New York

Library of Congress Cataloging in Publication Data

Turnbull, Patrick.
  Solferino, the birth of a nation.

  1. Solferino, Battle of, 1859.   2. Italy—History—
1849-1870.   I. Title.
DG554.5.S7T87   1985   945'.08   85-10906
ISBN 0-312-74573-7

First published in Great Britain by Robert Hale Ltd.

First U.S. Edition

10 9 8 7 6 5 4 3 2 1

Contents

Illustrations

Part One
THE THORNY PATH

1

The House of Savoy

Italy, the country which for centuries, as the centre of the Roman Empire, had ruled the then known world, ceased to be a united, independent nation when its vast domains were invaded, dismembered and overrun by wave after converging wave of 'barbarians' from the north and east. Pietro Orsi, a noted professor of Padua University in the early years of the present century, insists that one of the saddest days of history was 'that of the year 568 on which the King of the Lombards, Alboin, from the heights of the Julian Alps, looked down upon the rich provinces that were to be the prey of his people ...'. It was the end of 'The Glory that was Rome', for with the eventual ebb of the barbarian tide, once all-powerful Italy would be relegated to the humiliating role of being hacked up into a cluster of mini-states, each one a pawn in the long struggles of 'major' powers for European hegemony.

By the middle of the eighteenth century, there were eight of these mini-states: the kingdom of Naples and Sicily, the kingdom of Sardinia, which included Piedmont and Savoy, and the city of Nice, the Papal States, the republics of Genoa and Venice, the grand duchy of Tuscany, and the duchies of Parma and Modena. Yet in spite of the political chaos, it was at this time that a reviving spirit of national awareness, a whisper of nostalgia for a great past, began to make a timid reappearance.

This emerging hope was first voiced by the poets Vittorio Alfieri (1749-1803) and Giuseppe Parini (1729-99) finding an echo not so much in the hearts of the aristocracy but in those of a new social phenomenon, the middle class which had come into being thanks to the upsurge of industry and commerce in

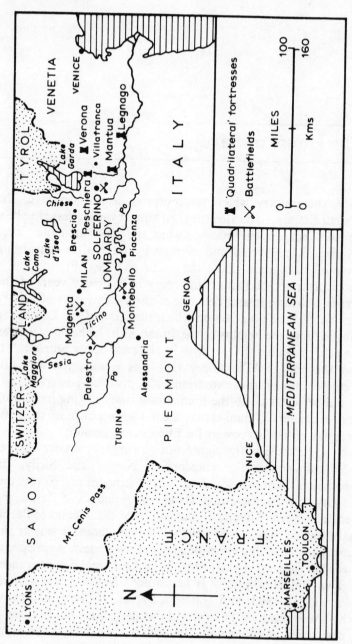

the north. Unfortunately this spiritual revival of an almost forgotten patriotism only served initially to widen the gulf existing between the states, as rulers and the upper classes of the rural areas looked with suspicion and hostility on the growth of these 'modern' ideas which they saw as a threat to their age-old privileges.

The French Revolution was greeted with modest enthusiasm in the north, an approbation which grew steadily to explode in rapturous welcome as the first French troops entered the country. Soon the people of Reggio and Modena had expelled their ducal rulers to unite with Bologna and Ferrara, captured by the French from the Papal States, to form the Cispadane Republic.

On 7 January 1797 the Cispadane Congress officially adopted a new standard. There was something prophetic in this gesture, for the standard would one day become the national flag of Italy. In honour of the French it was a tricolor, and as on that of revolutionary France two of the bands were white and red. But instead of blue, the third was green, 'a colour already familiar in local military equipment'.

Even when General Bonaparte became the Emperor Napoleon I, the hopes of Italian patriots remained pinned on France. The Emperor, being of Italian origin, was at heart in sympathy with Italian aspirations but, nevertheless, always thought of the country as a favourite vassal or even as an integral part of France. It was he who decreed that the peninsula be divided into three provinces. North-eastern Italy and Rome were to be a department of the French Empire. Lombardy, Venice, Reggio, Modena, the Romagna and the Marches were to be united to form the kingdom of Italy whose king would be Napoleon himself, his stepson Eugène de Beauharnais being nominated viceroy. The third province was to be the kingdom of Naples, ruled at first by Napoleon's brother Joseph, later by Marshal Joachim Murat, the famous light cavalry leader, husband of Napoleon's sister Caroline.

Though grieved by such total French domination, the Italians were able to persuade themselves that it was but a temporary measure before a gradual hand-over of power. As a result, 'the reawakening of Italian life was prodigious.

Magnificent streets were opened; commerce and industry were favoured, agriculture encouraged. Learning was promoted, monuments erected ... thus grew up a new generation destined to accomplish the great work of the Italian revival.'

This seemingly bright future was blighted in 1814 when the French Empire was overthrown, the Allies entered Paris, and Napoleon was banished to the little isle of Elba. In Italy only Murat remained, having quarrelled with his brother-in-law, as a reminder of French influence. Yet it was not long before he felt his position to be tenuous in the extreme. As soon as he heard of Napoleon's landing at Cannes, and hoping to profit by the spirit of independence which he believed to be stronger than ever, he launched an appeal to all Italians to join him in a war to free their land of the foreigner, and on 15 March 1815 led an army northwards.

Though a brilliant cavalry leader, Murat was no strategist. Furthermore the Italians were not so sure that he could be trusted. They suspected that his fervently expressed pan-Italian sentiments were nothing but a cloak hiding his true purpose: the protection and preservation of his own privileges. He pursued his advance as far as the Po, but the country did not rally to him as he had hoped; in fact his army was beginning to dwindle. News then reached him that a sea-borne invasion of Naples was imminent, whereupon he turned about, the Austrians hard on his heels. On 2 and 3 May, at the battle of Tolentino, he was outmanoeuvred and decisively defeated by a one-eyed Austrian, General Adam von Neipperg, who had become in the meantime the lover of Napoleon's second wife, Marie Louise, eldest daughter of the Austrian Emperor Francis I.

Murat fled to Corsica, and on 9 June the Austrian puppet Ferdinand of Bourbon was again King of Naples.

Murat's fate was perhaps more pathetic than tragic. In spite of the total elimination of French influence after Waterloo, he made a last desperate attempt to regain his kingdom, sailing from the Corsican port of Ajaccio with a bare 250 followers. Bad weather dispersed his little fleet so that, when he set foot on Italian soil at Pizzo in Calabria, his army was reduced to a grand total of nineteen. Rejected by the people of

Pizzo, he was heading for the village of Monteleone when he and his band were surrounded. Arrested, he was shut up in the local *castello*. Tried by a military tribunal a few days later, he was condemned to death and shot that same afternoon. He died as he had lived: bravely. His only complaint was that the firing squad detailed to execute an ex-king and a Marshal of France should be commanded by a mere captain.

The Congress of Vienna, moulded by Metternich, the ultra-traditionalist Austrian Chancellor, produced yet another mutilated version of Italy. Austria swallowed up Lombardy and the former republic of Venice, which were to be called 'the kingdom of Lombardy-Venetia' and governed by a viceroy, the Archduke Rainer, brother of the Austrian Emperor, Francis I, while the duchy of Parma and Piacenza passed to Francis's daughter the ex-Empress of France, Marie Louise, who was soon happily installed in the city of Parma, with her lover Adam von Neipperg acting as 'adviser'. Modena also came under the aegis of Vienna, as did Tuscany, while the Pope, Pius VII, regained control of the Papal States. This meant that the only area of the peninsula to be ruled by an Italian was the kingdom of Piedmont and Sardinia, whose territory had been increased by the annexation of the Genoese Republic. Its capital was Turin, its monarch Victor Emmanuel I of the House of Savoy, who, being the father of four daughters, was obliged to recognize his childless brother, Charles Felix, as heir presumptive, since the Sardinian succession was governed by the Salic Law.

The situation was further complicated by the fact that if, by the time of his death, Charles Felix was still without a male offspring, the royal line would be continued by a branch of the family, that of Savoy-Carignano, represented by a young man of sixteen, Charles Albert, whose father had died when the boy was only two years old.

The prospect of a united Italy seemed very remote, even though a prophetic utterance had been made by the imperial prisoner on St. Helena. 'Italy', said Napoleon, 'seems destined to form a great and important nation. Unity of language, customs and literature will lead, in the more or less distant future, to a union of the inhabitants under one single government ... it is beyond doubt that the Italians will one day make Rome their seat of government.'

The first mutterings of the people to hint that such a prophecy might well be realized came in the year 1820 and appeared to be more of a political than a national movement. Thanks to the influence of Metternich, liberal rule introduced during the days of French domination had been replaced by uncompromising absolutism. Thus when two revolutions shook Naples and Piedmont, sparked off by members of a secret society, the Carbonari,* the leaders made no mention of unity or driving out the foreigner but declared their objective to be the overthrow of absolute government and the setting up of a 'liberal' constitution.

In Naples, thanks to prompt Austrian intervention, the uprising was speedily suppressed, and from then on Ferdinand was able to enforce the Vienna line with the aid of a strong Austrian garrison. In Piedmont, however, matters were considerably more complicated. The Carbonari made it clear that they wanted to drive out not Victor Emmanuel himself but his 'reactionary' entourage. Their wish was to see a constitution set up, and for this to be followed by a declaration of war on Austria. In addition they were counting on the backing of the young heir presumptive, Charles Albert, believed to be full of youthful enthusiasm for liberal ideals.

To begin with, the uprising obtained some considerable measure of success. The garrison of Alessandria, second city of the kingdom, rallied to the cause and was unshaken by the news of a heavy defeat suffered by their comrades at Rieti, near Naples. The Turin garrison in turn hailed the revolution and went as far as to threaten to bombard the city if the Carbonari demands were not met.

---

* The founder of the society known as the Carbonari, whose original objective was to resist French occupation in the 1790s, was a native of Tuscany, Filippo Buonarroti. Being in no way anti-clerical, they called themselves after their patron saint, St Theobald, the charcoal-maker. In the early days members took to the mountains and, to cloak their subversive activities, pretended to be charcoal-burners (*carbonari*). At its height the society counted over a quarter of a million members drawn from all ranks of society and every profession. Their colours were black, blue and red: black for charcoal and faith, blue for smoke and hope, red for fire and charity.

Though a kindly man, Victor Emmanuel was, at heart, a despot. On his re-entering Turin after the fall of the Napoleonic Empire, the pre-1798 régime had been rigorously re-established. It was for this reason that not only middle-class liberals but many of the ruling families felt that the kingdom should be looking to the future, and the King himself be replaced by a younger, more dynamic individual with a more modern outlook. Nor did they feel that Charles Felix filled the role. Charles Albert, on the other hand, young, tall, handsome, making no secret of his 'advanced' political views, seemed the ideal candidate. All Turin was fond of quoting how, after a demonstration followed by a 'sit-in' at the university, he had not only visited imprisoned students but sent them food parcels and gifts of money.

It was while the rebels were waiting for the King's answer that one of the ringleaders, Commandante Santorra di Santarosa, accompanied by three brother officers presented himself at Charles Albert's residence, the Palazzo Carignano, where they were joined by another leader, the Marquis Roberto d'Azeglio. Admitted to the Prince's presence, they proceeded to lay before him their detailed plan of action, which, they stressed, was in no way against the monarchy but a genuine attempt to open the King's eyes to the reality of the situation, begging him to grant the constitution demanded and to speed to the assistance of their persecuted 'brothers' in the south.

They then implored Charles Albert, for the sake of the country, to place himself at the head of the movement.

There are two directly opposing versions of what exactly took place during this meeting: that of Charles Albert himself and that of Santarosa. The latter insisted that 'the Prince agreed to everything and welcomed the right to act as mediator between the insurgents and the King'. This Charles Albert denied vigorously; far from agreeing with the conspirators, he claimed that he did everything in his power to persuade them to abandon the plan and not to dishonour the oath of loyalty they had sworn to the Crown. No one is in a firm position to assert which version is the true one. All that one knows is that the green, red and white tricolor, looked upon as a revolutionary standard, was raised in both Turin and Alessandria the following day.

From that moment events moved rapidly. Victor Emmanuel was no fighter, but he would not be bullied into granting a constitution, nor would he contemplate a trial of strength; for him the line of least resistance.

On 13 March he startled Turin by the announcement of his abdication in favour of his brother Charles Felix. But since the latter was then on a visit to Modena, he appointed the twenty-three-year-old Charles Albert regent until the new King's return. The moment the act had been signed, Victor Emmanuel left troubled Turin for the more peaceful atmosphere of Nice.

It was an agonizing moment for the young Regent – and one cannot help feeling a degree of contempt for Victor Emmanuel's deliberate shirking of responsibility – torn as he was between the loyalty to the throne and his own liberal beliefs. In the end, it was his private sentiments which won the day. After twelve hours of intense inner conflict, he bowed to popular will. The morning of 14 March saw the signing of a constitution similar to that which had been signed in Spain the previous year.

Charles Felix, however, was of tougher fibre than his brother. When news of the *coup d'état* reached him in Modena, he reacted swiftly. The constitution was immediately repudiated. All those who had taken part were declared *hors la loi*, thus automatically facing the death penalty. The Regent was ordered to leave the capital immediately.

Shattered by a profound sense of personal failure and by the sudden revelation – or so it seemed to him – of the enormity of his crime, Charles Albert obeyed without questioning, leaving Santarosa, promoted Minister of War, to try to save the situation.

When it came to protecting his interests, Charles Felix was without scruples. He had no qualms about invoking the aid of the traditional enemy, Austria. Santarosa and his constitutionalists, who had determined to fight, found themselves facing impossible odds. Even with their own people they were in the minority. Theoretically the constitution was popular with the masses, but both Victor Emmanuel and Charles Felix were well liked by their subjects as individuals, so much so that, when matters reached a head, the counter-revolutionary element in the army outnumbered the conspirators by at least two to one. When the ranks of his opponents were swelled by a small but efficient Austrian contingent, Santarosa realized that he was lost.

Though neither a brilliant nor an inspired leader, he was not lacking in courage. Rather than surrender he preferred to go down fighting. The two forces met at Novara on 7 April. Forced to fall back before superior numbers and a far heavier weight of artillery, the constitutionalists' retreat degenerated into a rout offering little or no resistance to repeated charges by the Austrian cavalry. The King's army entered Alessandria and Turin in triumph, but, strangely enough, once victory had been won and the rising decisively crushed, Charles Felix showed himself in no great hurry to assume the throne, preferring to return to Modena, where he remained till October.

The defeats in Naples and Piedmont spelled a temporary halt to Italian aspirations. Many Piedmontese were happy to call the Austrians their friends and join in a witch-hunt for 'liberals', intellectuals and revolutionaries. Only Britain, eternal sentimental supporter of the 'underdog', of all the countries of Europe, sympathized with the Carbonari, offering a haven for political exiles, among them the Neapolitan poet Gabriele Rosetti and Antonio Panizzi, the well-known scholar who eventually became senior librarian of the British Museum.

The unfortunate Charles Albert was looked upon as the villain by both sides. The King and the loyalists considered him a renegade. They refused to believe that he had been motivated by anything but a lust for personal power, that seeing, as it were, the throne before his eyes for the taking, he was not prepared to wait for time to remove the two brothers who stood in his path. Ambition, therefore, had led him to betray his family – had turned him into a royal Judas.

For their part the constitutionalists were convinced that his professed sympathy for their cause was all part of a plot to use his position as a bait, that indeed he had been acting as an *agent provocateur*, his role to induce Santarosa and other leaders to divulge their plans, which could thus be the more easily countered.

For a time it was thought that Charles Felix was so outraged that he envisaged his cousin's arrest, trial and subsequent execution for high treason. But having dismissed such a procedure as over-dramatic, he was determined to deny him his rights of succession. To do so, however, meant revoking the Salic Law, thus flouting the principle of 'legitimacy' so dear to Europe's reigning houses. It was for this reason that, at the moment it appeared that Charles Albert had thrown away his future, he found a most unexpected ally in the person of Metternich, in whose eyes legitimacy was 'all the law and the prophets'.

Furthermore, Charles Albert's behaviour both before and after the crisis suggested a young man vacillating and easily led, and the last thing the Austrian Chancellor wished to see was a strong man directing Piedmont's destiny and casting nationalistic eyes on Austrian-ruled Lombardy and Venetia. Charles Albert, therefore, must not be disinherited. Much to his fury, Charles Felix received a communication from Vienna to the effect that 'no material proof existed against the Prince of Carignano which could justify so drastic a step as overriding the laws of succession'.

The communication constituted a blatant, unwarranted interference by a foreign power in Piedmont's domestic affairs. But at that time one could not afford to snub Metternich; his dictate had to be accepted.

Nothing, however, could prevent Charles Felix from insisting that the erring cousin atone in a certain measure for his alleged crime. Louis XVIII of France was about to despatch an expeditionary force to Spain to help Ferdinand VII throw off the chains of the constitution imposed on him, much against his will, in 1820. Charles Albert was ordered to march with the French and seek his redemption – hopefully his death as far as Charles Felix was concerned – on the battlefield.

The unhappy ex-Regent needed no persuading. The events leading to his disgrace had left him with an incurable moral ailment. Until the failed *coup*, he had, as has been said, been a cheerful, carefree young man with a roving eye not always appreciated by his prim Austrian wife. Very much a man's man, he enjoyed drinking and gaming in the company of officers of his own age, happy also to accompany them on nocturnal adventures liable to end up with some gallant rendezvous with the ladies of the town.

But from March 1821 his entire attitude to life changed.

Guilt complexes weighed him down. If there were to be a future, he felt that he must first expiate his crime, cleansing his soul of the blood of those who fell at Novara and later in the limited purge ordered by Charles Felix. From the day he left Turin, he was seldom, if ever, seen to smile. Morose, introspective, there were times when those near him feared that he was bent on taking his own life. No call to arms was ever more eagerly answered.

The campaign was brief. As had been expected, Charles Albert displayed outstanding bravery under fire. At a reception held at the Tuileries after the expeditionary force's return, its mission successfully accomplished, Louis XVIII embraced him, saying, 'You have shown the world that Piedmont will have one day a king who is a valliant soldier whom I both love and esteem'. With such a mark of favour from one of Europe's most influential figures, and with Metternich's semi-official blessing, Charles Albert was allowed to return to his country estates in Piedmont. It was not a very happy return. Charles Felix was frankly disappointed to see his cousin still in the land of the living. There was no public reconciliation. But Charles Albert made it very evident that he had no intention of giving the King any cause for worry. From the moment of his return he buried himself in the country, leading an existence more befitting a man in retirement than a young prince on whose shoulders the cares of state were destined to fall. Gone for ever was the dashing youth, the young man of the world, to be replaced by the sombre recluse.

In all this turmoil, one event which was to have lasting repercussions on Italian history passed almost unnoticed. In 1820 Charles Albert's wife, Theresa of Hapsburg-Tuscany, gave birth to her eldest child, a boy christened Victor Emmanuel, who would become not only the eighth king of Sardinia and Piedmont but the first king of Italy.

Comparative quiet succeeded chaos for almost a decade, until 1830. In that year there were uprisings in the Papal States, in Bologna, Parma and Modena. They aroused no nostalgic echoes in Charles Albert's heart. The very few public utterances made by him condemned all forms of revolution, and in particular the Paris *coup d'état* by which Charles X was forced to cede his throne to Louis Philippe of Orleans. And as was to be expected, Charles Felix made no attempt to succour his 'brother' Italians as once more their attempts to throw off the foreign yoke were crushed by Austrian military power.

Suddenly, in April 1831, Charles Felix died, and Charles Albert, still a comparatively young man, mounted the throne so ardently desired in early youth. In spirit, however, it was a very different Charles Albert. From the moment of his return to Turin, he made it clear that, for the rest of his life, he would be a staunch upholder of Church and State based on the foundation of absolutism. There were those who hoped that, once crowned, Charles Albert might revert to his youthful ideals, grant a constitution and declare an anti-Austrian crusade, but when it became evident that such dreams were idle, the liberal, republican sympathizers, whose influence had been growing in secret, came out into the open to avow their intention of destroying absolutism and with it the system of monarchy, now as unpopular as foreign rule.

The liberal mouthpiece was a certain Giuseppe Mazzini, whose inflammatory oratory and pamphlets composed with a rare literary virtuosity had fired not only Italians but liberals throughout the world. Determined to do away with the power of Pope and monarchs alike, and to create a United Republic of Italy, Mazzini founded a society known as *Giovine Italia* (Young Italy) which supplanted the now decadent Carbonari.

Despite his ferocious condemnation of kings, Mazzini sent Charles Albert an 'open letter' soon after the coronation. In it he employed a mixture of flattery and menace. Charles Albert's youthful liberalism was praised. He was then begged 'to restore a constitution in Piedmont' prior to marching against the Austrians. 'Place yourself at the head of the nation,' Mazzini went on. 'Write on your flags – Union, Liberty, Independence. Free Italy from the barbarian. Your safety lies at the sword's point. Draw it and throw away the scabbard.' He ended with a warning: 'If you do not act, others will: without you and against you!'

Charles Albert did not reply. Far from awakening latent memories, the letter infuriated him. No secret society, he declared, would be tolerated in his domains. Mazzini, who was then in France, was warned that from then on he would be regarded as *persona non grata* in Piedmont. Imprisonment, possibly execution, awaited him if he ever returned to his homeland. Soon afterwards this threat was crystallized by his trial *in absentia* naming him *hors la loi*. On hearing of this he moved from France to the comparative safety of exile in Britain.

About this time another voice, later to be one of the best known of the century, was beginning to make itself heard: that of Count Camillo Benso di Cavour, second son of the Marquis of Cavour, who, after a brief army career, had turned to politics. Cavour considered himself a liberal but, unlike Mazzini, favoured a liberal monarchy rather than a republic. A man of unlimited ambition, he was soon admitting freely that his ultimate goal was to become 'the First Minister of the First King of Italy,' a statement which did not endear him to either Metternich or the Austrian Ambassador in Turin.

Hard working, genuinely concerned with his people's good, Charles Albert gradually began to win back a measure of respect and love. He 'wanted to be the most benevolent of despots at the same time as he hated the idea of being the most undemocratic of democrats'. He was also, in the early days of his reign, a shrewd judge of his fellow men and able to pick capable subordinates. Under his direct control, he gathered together a highly efficient team of ministers, with the result that, within a few years of his accession, Piedmont was universally recognized as the best run and most prosperous of the Italian states. This fact acted as an irritant to the neighbouring Austrian puppet rulers, and indeed to Vienna, but it was part of Charles Albert's policy to remain on good terms with his powerful neighbour, and he noted with considerable concern that border clashes seemed to be on the increase, the majority of them Austrian provoked.

This was not his only worry. In spite of his growing personal popularity, there were still die-hards from all ranks of society who regarded him as the traitor of 1821. The principle of assassination, heritage of the Borgias, was openly recognized in Italy, and Charles Albert was fond of saying, half jokingly, half plaintively, that he lived his life between 'the threat of the dagger of the Carbonari and the chocolates of the Jesuits'.

Nevertheless, some fourteen years elapsed before the unrest simmering at the time of his accession seemed to be again on the point of coming to boiling point. Sporadic uprisings broke out, though as before the Austrian iron fist was able to crush any anti-governmental move in its infancy. In 1847, however, Pope Pius IX brought renewed hope to the liberal cause when he ordered the release of all those who had been incarcerated for political reasons on the instigation of his predecessor Gregory XVI. This decree, however, merely led to stricter police measures in Lombardy and in Tuscany, which in the latter verged on persecution. Stories of police brutality deeply moved Charles Albert, reawakening a sense of patriotism which seemed to have been crushed at the moment of his disgrace in 1821, so much so that he began to throw out hints that he might well be contemplating that much talked-of War of Independence and that, if indeed he did give the order to march, the Piedmontese army would find him at its head. Very shortly after allowing these rumours to circulate, he received a visit from Lord Minto, officially representing the British Government, who advised him 'to grant large reforms and free himself from reactionary counsellors'.

Such advice from the spokesman of so powerful a nation had an immediate effect.

On 30 October a royal decree announced forthcoming free elections of communal and provincial committees, a restriction of police powers, and a large measure of freedom of the Press. This latest concession was marked by the publication of Piedmont's first independent political newspaper, *Il Risorgimento*, its founder and editor Camillo di Cavour.

The general atmosphere was electric as 1847 drew to its close.

In Venice there were violent protests against vigorous Press censorship. there were riots over such seeming trivialities as the price of state-controlled tobacco in the Lombard capital, Milan. There were massive demonstrations of a nationalist nature in the streets of Pavia and Padua. Scenting the possibility of still more serious trouble to come, the Austrians strongly reinforced their Italian garrisons, sending the octogenerian Marshal Radetsky, despite his age one of the most professionally skilled and physically vigorous military leaders of the day, as overall commander.

2
The Years of Despair

In 1848, 'The Year of Revolutions', the tide of insurgency swept not only Italy but most of Europe. In France, King Louis Philippe was toppled from his throne to make way for the Second Republic. In Austria, the young prince Franz came to power as the Emperor Franz Josef, to begin the longest reign in European history, after Vienna had been taken over by mob rule and the Court had been obliged to flee first to Innsbruck, then to Olmutz. The whole of the Italian peninsula was racked by the struggle waged by those who felt that foreign domination of their homeland was no longer tolerable.

At the time, the three main centres of turmoil in western Europe appeared to be entirely individual and unlinked, yet each was to exercise a vital influence on Italy's destiny. These widespread events and their sequel were to converge inexorably eleven years later, to culminate in the mighty drama whose final act was constituted by the battle of Solferino, a forerunner of the slaughter to come during the years 1914-18.

In Piedmont Charles Albert was continuing his policy of cautious reform. In March the constitution which had provoked his fall from grace seventeen years earlier was granted. Within a few days came news that the city of Milan had risen in mass revolt against the Austrian garrison, an event which would come to be spoken of as 'The Five Glorious Days'.

For a parallel in modern times one might cite the 1944 Warsaw uprising against the Germans, but with this difference: in 1848 it was the insurgents who gained the day, albeit temporarily. After five days of bloody street fighting in which no quarter was given by either side, Marshal Radetsky came to the conclusion that, for the time being at any rate, the close house-to-house battle being waged in the city's maze of streets could only be to his disadvantage. He therefore withdrew his troops eastwards, across the Mincio river to an area dubbed the 'Quadrilateral', a roughly square-shaped strip of territory whose western defence was the line of the Mincio river, its four corners formed by the heavily fortified towns of Peschiera, Verona, Legnago and Mantua.

The effect of this victory of untrained civilians over disciplined regular battalions, resulting in the liberation of the Lombard capital, reverberated throughout the peninsula. Surely, nationalists argued, this was the moment to raise the flag of independence, the tricolor, the length and breadth of the country, especially as news was coming through of the parallel victory of the mob in Vienna, the arch enemy Metternich's downfall and the imperial flight from the capital. It was seized upon by Cavour, whose leading article in *Il Risorgimento* on 22 March proclaimed that circumstances had combined to offer a unique opportunity to smash the Austrian hold. 'One way alone', wrote Cavour, 'is open for the nation, the government, the King. War! Immediate war!'

If it can be argued that Charles Albert's tergiversation, his inability to reach a speedy decision, had brought about his downfall in 1821, one may insist all the more that his failure to respond without second thoughts to this call for action produced even more deleterious effects: ruinous military defeat, the humiliation of Piedmont, his own ignominious exit from the scene, to be followed shortly afterwards by death under the shadow of personal disgrace in self-imposed exile. He had already become known in some circles as '*il re tentenna*' ('the wavering king'). He now proceeded to justify this far from flattering title.

Mobilization was criminally slow. It was not till the end of the month that the army was ready to march. By then the energetic Radetsky had made his dispositions on the battlefield of his own choosing, where he waited, supremely confident that he could defeat the Piedmontese and any allies they might pick up *en route*, should they venture to attack him.

On paper Charles Albert had assembled a formidable force.

The Piedmontese had mobilized seventy thousand men. This number was swelled by patriot groups from western Lombardy, levies from Tuscany and sixteen thousand Neapolitans, bringing the grand total to close on a hundred thousand. Against this mass Radetsky could muster only some forty thousand. Yet despite his reverse at the hands of Milan's citizens, he had so poor an opinion of the standard of Piedmontese training and of their commanders that he never doubted that victory would smile on him the day the two armies met in formal battle.

As an individual, Charles Albert had indeed shown conspicuous gallantry during the Spanish campaign. Now he displayed equally outstanding inefficiency as commander of an army. Though unopposed, the advance across Lombardy was unbelievably dragged out. Crawling forward, the Piedmontese did not reach the Mincio till late April.

It was Radetsky's plan to lure Charles Albert into the centre of the Quadrilateral as, on an infinitely greater scale, Czar Alexander I had lured Napoleon into the heart of Russia in 1812. The crossing of the Mincio was nowhere contested, and it was not till 2 May that there occurred a minor encounter at Pastrengo on the east bank in which the Piedmontese suffered considerably heavier losses than their opponents – 866 killed and wounded as against 162. This was followed by the battle of Santa Lucia on the 6th, a serious reverse for the Piedmontese in spite of the fact that they enjoyed a two-to-one numerical superiority.

At the end of the month Charles Albert gained his only tactical success, when the Piedmontese, who had invested the Quadrilateral's north-west bastion, Peschiera, defeated an Austrian relief column at Goito, whereupon the Peschiera garrison surrendered. This local victory was exaggerated out of all proportion. Jubilant Italians were convinced that the campaign was won, independence round the corner. Charles Albert was cheered as King of Italy.

Deception soon followed. Radetsky was unperturbed by Peschiera's fall. Two days later, reinforcements in the form of thirty thousand Austrian regular troops under the command of General Nugent, arrived on the scene after a rapid march from

Venice. Charles Albert's dilatoriness had destroyed whatever slender hope of victory he might have had had he struck hard and immediately at the enemy, badly shaken momentarily by the setback of the 'Five Glorious Days'.

As soon as Nugent's column had concentrated on the outskirts of Verona, Radetsky staged a lightning attack on a detached Piedmontese division commanded by one of Piedmont's more able generals, Giovanni Durando, bivouacked in the fields outside Vicenza. The division contained a high proportion of levies from Tuscany and the Papal States who fought with great courage but were no match for the better-trained Austrians. Soon their casualties had mounted to pass the two thousand mark, whereupon Durando, despairing of being able to fight his way out of the encircling ring, surrendered.

News of this disaster effectively dissipated the euphoria following on Peschiera's fall. Again Charles Albert wavered, unable to make up his mind as to whether he should pursue the offensive, despite the loss of an entire division, or fall back and consolidate his hold on Milan and western Lombardy. He did neither. After wasting days in indeterminate manoeuvring, he grouped his entire force in the neighbourhood of Custozza, almost in the centre of the Quadrilateral, thereby playing straight into Radetsky's hands.

Battle was joined on 23 July and lasted three days. Once again Piedmontese courage proved of no avail against better Austrian training and infinitely superior leadership. On the 26th Charles Albert ordered a general retreat to the west of the Mincio, still hoping that, despite his heavy losses, he would be able to organize Milan as an impregnable fortress. By the time the last Piedmontese soldier was back over the river, by the end of the following day, 25,000 dead, seriously wounded and prisoners had been left behind.

The road to Milan was covered in four days – that is to say, in exactly one quarter of the time of the advance. Unfortunately for Charles Albert, the citizens of the Lombard capital were no longer motivated by the fervour of the 'Five Glorious Days'. In the interim they had had the time to ponder on their enormous losses and the devastating material damage to their beloved city which had been the price of their triumph. Now, learning of the failure of the much-heralded Piedmontese offensive, they were inclined to qualify their own victory as Pyrrhic and had no wish to expose themselves to a repetition of the horrors which it had entailed.

Nevertheless, Charles Albert, continuing his monumental errors of judgement, insisted on bringing his dispirited men within the illusory shelter of the city walls and then allowed himself to be boxed up, the enemy without and within a population whose sentiments had swung from near idolization to contempt and near hatred. In so hopeless a position, he had no alternative but to beg Radetsky for an armistice.

The old Marshal, his army still numerically inferior and awaiting further reinforcements, was wise enough not to try to impose humiliating terms. All he demanded was a return to the *status quo ante* 17 March. The Piedmontese were to withdraw immediately across the Ticino river, leaving the Austrians to re-occupy Milan and the Lombard plain. Elsewhere Italian resistance was being stamped out by the better-equipped, better-organized Austrians, though for a few months the Venetians, who had proclaimed themselves an independent republic, would be able to carry on a forlorn fight aided by the natural defences afforded by the lagoons. Naples and the duchies were once more subject states, while a rebellion in Sicily had been crushed with such brutality that it had aroused international protest.

Despite the bitter disappointment reigning in Piedmont itself, there were isolated reasons for tempered satisfaction, especially in the fact that, though defeated, Piedmontese courage on the battlefield constituted an honourable defeat. Custozza was talked of as a 'temporary setback' and had in no way subdued the determination to continue the struggle when a suitable occasion was offered. The flock of volunteers from neighbouring states had been encouraging, even if their offers had not been turned to profit. Very unwisely, however, the King had rejected the offer of the services of the Nice-born patriot Giuseppe Garibaldi, who had just returned from South America, because of his well-known liberal, republican views. 'To make such a man a general' said Charles Albert, 'would be dishonouring to the enemy.'

One factor had been much in evidence: leadership, organization and staff work had touched abysmal depths of ineptitude. In nine cases out of ten, orders had been confused and contradictory. In the whole army, it was said, there was only one map of the area east of the Chiese river. Medical care, never a characteristic of mid-nineteenth-century campaigns, had been non-existent. Within days fever and dysentery were decimating the ranks; a badly wounded man – and many not so gravely wounded – had little or no hope of survival.

The King and his subordinate commanders had been out-generalled and out-manoeuvred at every turn – with one notable exception.

The twenty-eight-year-old heir to the throne, Victor Emmanuel, had commanded a division, and during the whole campaign, and particularly at Custozza, he had shown the same degree of personal courage his father had shown in Spain. Indeed, he had done more than just prove himself to be a brave man. It was his division which formed the rearguard during the retreat to Milan, and though the men were depressed by failure, severely shaken by the heavy casualties suffered, Victor Emmanuel was able to accomplish a near miracle.

No military manoeuvre is more difficult to carry out successfully than a retreat involving men whose morale has been sapped by defeat and lack of confidence in their leaders. The least unfortunate incident can turn an ordered withdrawal into a disorderly rout, a *sauve qui peut*, especially when the pursuers are strong in cavalry, as were the Austrians. However, though constantly harried by Radetsky's vanguard and set upon by swarms of hussars waiting to cut off stragglers as the Cossacks had done when the *Grande Armée* fell back from Moscow in 1812, Victor Emmanuel managed to hold together his weary, dispirited battalions, inspiring them by his personal example. On several occasions determined efforts to smash through the rearguard to fall on the straggling main body were not only decisively repulsed but routed by counter-attacks under his leadership.

It was the first time the heir to the throne had been permitted to play a prominent role in the country's affairs, and he had emerged with flying colours.

The campaign aroused great interest throughout Europe. Generally speaking, public sympathy lay with the Piedmontese. The British, mesmerized by the spectacle of the Piedmontese David confronting the Austrian Goliath, went as far as to offer help. But by then Charles Albert had become a confirmed xenophobe. Though he was diplomat enough to proffer thanks, the offer was brushed aside by the rather churlish remark '*Italia farà da sę*' ('Italy will manage on her own') – subsequently to be the only one of his public utterances to be recorded in history. One must at the same time admire his determination to pursue an aim in spite of rebuffs and failures, for, once back in Turin, he made it clear that he was treating the armistice as an expediency, a mere temporary suspension of hostilities.

He was also honest enough to admit to himself that he must bear the lion's share for the disastrous handling of the army, above all the failure to strike while the Austrians still reeled from the blow dealt them by the Milan uprising, and to profit by the opportunities offered by crushing numerical superiority. He saw, indeed, that if he retained supreme command, it must be in name only, that for the sake of Piedmont's very existence, were war to be renewed, a military brain capable of challenging Radetsky must be found.

One wonders whether it was the strange, almost traditional, jealousy which seemed to poison the relationship between so many monarchs and their sons – and in particular their direct heirs – which made Charles Albert ignore the one man combining natural tactical flair with personal charisma and that capability of inspiring men to accept the worse hardships, even death: his son Victor Emmanuel. It might have been jealousy, or again it might have been the fear of being accused of nepotism, but this obvious choice was passed by. Instead he picked on an elderly Polish officer, veteran of the Napoleonic wars, living in Piedmont, Albert Czarnowsky, who with some difficulty was persuaded to take on the task of leading the Piedmontese army in the contemplated war of revenge. Czarnowsky had pointed out that being a foreigner and with a name almost impossible for anyone but a Pole to pronounce or write, his direction of operations must be behind the scenes. For the sake of morale and national pride, the army must appear to be led by some popular figure, while he himself took the field discreetly with the title of Chief of Staff.

Charles Albert agreed, yet once again failed to make the obvious appointment. In liaison with the battle-experienced Pole, Victor Emmanuel might well have led Piedmont to victory, for the two men complemented each other perfectly. But still nagged by the memory of defeat, Charles Albert decided to assume titular command himself and, to make matters worse, he then nominated a highly inefficient officer, General Ramorino, noted for his republican sympathies, as his second-in-command, hoping by so doing to offer a sop to Liberal opinion.

Although the glaring weaknesses brought to light by the Custozza disaster were still fresh in everyone's mind, no serious effort was made to improve administration, organization or the general level of field training. 'The gunners', said a contemporary source, 'hardly knew how to load their guns; the infantry in large part actually remained in ignorance of how to use the percussion cap muskets with which most of them were armed.' It mattered little, therefore, that when Charles Albert decided that the time was ripe to re-open hostilities, his army had been officially quoted as reaching the impressive figure of 150,000 all ranks; the true fighting effective was probably nearer 55,000.

Further outbreaks against Austrian rule throughout Italy furnished Charles Albert with the excuse to renew the attempt to free Lombardy and expunge the bitter memories of the previous year. Determined to seize and retain the initiative, the Piedmontese army crossed the Ticino on 2 March without a formal declaration of war. This second campaign was to last a bare three weeks. It was brutal, bloody and, from the Piedmontese point of view, an even greater disaster than that of 1848.

The overall plan devised by Czarnowsky was sound: to hold in the south with a reinforced division, while striking at Milan via Magenta with the main body. Not having formed a favourable opinion of Ramorino's capabilities, Czarnowsky gave him charge of the holding force, thinking that a purely static defensive role would reduce to a minimum the danger of his ineptitude compromising the master plan.

As soon as the report of the Piedmontese move reached Radetsky at Pavia, where the bulk of the Austrian army was concentrated, he moved rapidly to cross the Ticino, aiming at the small town of Cava on the west bank. This was what Czarnowsky had anticipated. The Ticino was a difficult river to cross in the face of opposition, and he reckoned that Ramorino would have little trouble in denying the passage to the enemy, who, in the meantime, would be leaving the road to Milan open and thus dangerously exposing his right flank.

Unfortunately Ramorino allowed himself to be completely deceived by false intelligence concerning Austrian intentions. Ignoring his formal orders, he ferried his entire force over to the south bank of the Po and then began a slow, straggling march in an easterly direction. This idiotic manoeuvre created a wide gap through which the Austrians poured to overwhelm Cava before swinging north, then pushing rapidly towards Novara and Mortara.

As soon as news of Ramorino's fatal blunder and the Austrian advance reached Czarnowsky, he gave orders to face about and to re-cross the Ticino. But now, instead of holding the initiative, he was obliged to make frantic efforts to form some sort of *ad hoc* defence to meet the Austrian onslaught.

The first major clash took place at Mortara, in which the Piedmontese were driven from the field, falling back in some confusion on Novara.

On 22 March the final battle was engaged.

For Charles Albert the day marked the completion of the circle of misfortune which had begun on the same spot in 1821 with the defeat of the supporters of his hastily proclaimed constitution. As at Custozza the struggle was long, bitter and costly in lives. Once more Victor Emmanuel, accompanied by his younger brother, the Duke of Genoa, distinguished himself. At the head of the 21st Regiment of the Line, he led a charge which recaptured the vital central position of La Citadella, stormed by the Austrians at the beginning of the day. But elsewhere on the swaying front superior Austrian training and discipline were wearing down unco-ordinated Piedmontese courage. Though repeatedly assaulted, Victor Emmanuel's regiment was able to hold on to La Citadella, but at all other points the Austrians were gaining ground as Piedmontese defences gradually crumbled under remorseless pressure.

Seeing total defeat staring him in the face, Charles Albert endeavoured, as Napoleon had done in 1814, to seek death on the battlefield. On such occasions, though, Death is inclined to display a somewhat warped sense of humour by denying its embrace. Though constantly exposed to hails of bullets and with shells bursting all round him, Charles Albert was not even grazed. Turning to Czarnowsky, he exclaimed bitterly, 'All is lost, even honour', and a few minutes later he repeated the agonized words which had fallen from Napoleon's lips as he regained consciousness after the failure of his suicide attempt at Fontainebleau – 'Even death betrays me!'

By nightfall the whole Piedmontese army, with the exception of Victor Emmanuel's regiment, had disintegrated to nothing but a fleeing rabble spread over the countryside. Very reluctantly Charles Albert allowed himself to be led from the field, and then, before dawn, he despatched an envoy to Radetsky to plead for an armistice.

Radetsky, however, was in a far less accommodating mood than after Custozza. The terms he offered, or rather demanded, were harsh. The Duke of Savoy (Victor Emmanuel) was to be handed over as a hostage; all Piedmontese territory between the Ticino river and Alessandria was to be ceded to Austria; the Piedmontese army was to be disbanded immediately.

There was no question of renewing the fight, yet Charles Albert could not bring himself to accept the Austrian demands as they stood. There seemed to be only one hope. If he himself were to disappear from the scene, the Austrian commander, who had grown to look on him as an implacable enemy and the prime motivator of unrest, might unbend. That same night, calling a meeting of all senior officers, he expounded his theory, concluding with the words, 'Since I have not succeeded in finding death, I must carry out the final sacrifice for my people. I give up my crown and abdicate in favour of my son.'*

* Though he had not found a hero's death on the battlefield, Charles Albert did not survive for long. Making his way to Oporto, Portugal, he entered a monastery, dying in July.

A more tragic, unpropitious moment to mount a throne could scarcely be imagined. Victor Emmanuel, however, was apparently unperturbed by the chaos he had inherited; both morally and physically he was of the toughest fibre. Indeed, only so tough a man could have survived the tribulations of the early months of his reign. Obliged to sign a treaty from which only the clause regarding a royal hostage had been erased, he was called upon immediately to face bitter internal dissension and the open hostility of those who blamed the country's misfortunes on the monarchy. Parliament, with a total lack of realism, talked of carrying on the war, even though the army had ceased to exist as such, and also strenuously opposed the cession of Alessandria.

His first acts were aimed at appeasing public opinion. A proclamation was issued affirming his intention of maintaining the constitution, and promising to make the re-creation of the national army a priority. A new cabinet was formed, with General Delaunay, the National Guard Commander, as a stop-gap Prime Minister. Within a few weeks Delaunay was replaced by the Marquis Massimo d'Azeglio, brother of the 1821 conspirator Roberto d'Azeglio.

At this difficult stage, Mazzini unwittingly helped to establish the new King's doubtful popularity by staging a revolt in Genoa against the Turin government. By threatening still further dismemberment of the state of Piedmont, Mazzini roused considerable indignation, and General Ramorino was ordered to march at the head of a hastily assembled force to deal with the insurrection.

By entrusting the suppression of the revolt to a man whose stupidity had contributed so considerably to the catastrophe of the March campaign, Victor Emmanuel was displaying the great natural cunning which was to reveal itself as an integral part of his nature. On the surface he was giving the general a chance to redeem himself. The truth of the matter was not so straightforward. Ramorino was known to be anti-monarchist, a former member of the Carbonari who never bothered to conceal the fact that his political aim was the establishment of a republic. The command thrust upon him therefore placed him on the horns of a dilemma. Were he to refuse on ideological grounds, he could be accused of insubordination, even treason; yet in carrying out the task efficiently, he ran the risk of being held up as a traitor to his principles, a reactionary and oppressor of the people.

As he hesitated, torn by conflicting emotions, Victor Emmanuel, having obtained his objective, gave the command to an old and trusted soldier, General La Marmora, who set about the job with such rapidity and vigour that Genoa was overrun by the loyal troops before the rebellious citizens had had time to organize an effective resistance. Concerning this operation, one can read a rather naïve report that: 'The Sardinians pillaged a little, ravished a little, murdered a little, but on the whole exhibited a remarkable restraint. The movement ended in very little bad blood between Genoa and the rest of the country ...'

The crushing of the revolt was followed by the arrest of General Ramorino. He was tried for disobeying General Czarnowsky's directions to stand firm and oppose the crossing of the Ticino at all costs. The trial would seem to have been justified, but the delay in setting up the court is open to criticism. Ramorino's failure to comply with such implicit instructions had certainly been directly responsible for the defeat. Furthermore, when the consequence of his blunder became apparent, he made no effort whatsoever to retrieve the situation. While the Austrians advanced north and the battles of Mortara and Novara raged, he sat idly with his force of twenty thousand men on the far bank of the Po. The trial was brief. Romarino was found guilty of gross negligence of duty and with no extenuating circumstances. Execution by firing squad was carried out rapidly. Rough justice had been done, and the King had rid himself, legally, of a potentially dangerous conspirator.

The prompt repression of the Genoese republicans also helped Victor Emmanuel in his dealing with Radetsky. The Austrian commander was impressed by the King's handling of affairs and the speed with which he had reacted to the threat to his authority, making it clear that he had no intention of seeking popularity by pandering to the Left. It was therefore preferable that a monarch of his calibre should remain on

Piedmont's throne, rather than that the country should fall under the influence of such men as Mazzini, or even Garibaldi. Having reached this conclusion, Radetsky was prepared to waive the harsher clauses of the armistice which might damage the new King's growing prestige.

For his part, Victor Emmanuel was quick to perceive and take advantage of Radetsky's more conciliatory frame of mind. It is said that in the course of conversations with the old Marshal, while asserting his intention to put down ruthlessly any attempt by the Left to seize power, he also managed to convey the impression that he was on excellent terms with France's new leader, the Prince President, Louis Napoleon, who had been carried to power in the course of the 1848 political upheavals, and that his personal friendship was likely to be sealed officially by a treaty guaranteeing mutual aid in the face of aggression on the part of any third nation.

The result of these conversations was a very emasculated version of the post-Novara terms. All talk of a hostage or hostages was dropped. No territory would be ceded by Piedmont, though the city of Alessandria would be occupied by an Austrian garrison till the payment of the war indemnity fixed at the equivalent of £3 million sterling.

It was a personal triumph and one which the Piedmontese were quick to praise. In turn it was remarkable how rapidly the King was able to gauge his subjects' changing mood and make his popularity all the more assured by granting from time to time apparent concessions to mild liberalism, yet firmly retaining maximum authority in his grasp. Furthermore, he was soon to show that he had the ability to pick the right man for the right job, aided by his keen insight into human nature, unprejudiced by personal leanings or emotions. At no time was this gift better displayed than in his choice of Count Camillo di Cavour, later to prove himself one of the century's truly great statesmen, as his right-hand man. Although, basically, Victor Emmanuel and Cavour were temperamentally and ideologically poles apart, the link between them was forged by intense patriotism.

Within a year of his accession, the vast majority of Piedmontese were fully aware of their good fortune in being citizens of Victor Emmanuel's realm. Elsewhere in the peninsula, the suppression of latent nationalism was being carried out with a fanaticism and severity at times recalling the worst excesses of the Inquisition.

In Rome an expeditionary force under General Oudinot, son of the famous First Empire marshal, battled for two months with Garibaldi's volunteers to liquidate the Roman Republic which had been set up by force by Mazzini. Oudinot showed himself unequal to the task, and it was not until the experienced Marshal Vaillant took over command that French bayonets were able to restore the Pope's temporal power. In Lombardy and Venetia, Austrian authorities were ordering men and women suspected of harbouring nationalist sentiments to be flogged in the streets. Arbitrary imprisonment without trial, torture and hanging overshadowed daily life. Palmerston was heard to say that the Austrian ruling classes were 'the greatest brutes that ever called themselves by the undeserved name of civilized men'.

Reports of these atrocities strengthened Victor Emmanuel's resolve to 'free his country'. But, practical and clear-thinking, he realized that, before rushing into an anti-Austrian crusade, he must first be sure that his own house was in order, its foundation solid. Domestic harmony, he soon became convinced, could be ensured only by the creation of a majority formed by a coalition of level-headed anti-extremists, recruited from all shades of political opinion. In a country like Piedmont where political passions flared on the flimsiest of pretexts, such a solution savoured of the impractical, yet within two years few Piedmontese would be found who would be prepared to put party before country.

3

Cavour, Victor Emmanuel and Napoleon

At the time he spoke of his close friendship with France's ruler, Victor Emmanuel was indulging in what we would call 'wishful thinking'. No personal links had in fact been formed, though he was determined that they would be and that it would be with the help of France that the Italian dream would ultimatly be fulfilled.

There were sound reasons for these hopes.

The Bonapartes (Buonopartes) were of Italian origin, and after the Emperor's fall many of the family settled in Italy, including the Prince-President's father, Louis, ex-King of Holland, who after his separation from his wife Hortense, Napoleon's step-daughter, took up residence in Florence. His two sons, Napoleon Louis and Louis Napoleon – the latter now ruler of France, had both spent much of their childhood with their innumerable Italian friends and relations. Though the two brothers were separated when their parents' marriage finally broke up, Napoleon remaining with his father while Louis resided with his mother on her Swiss estate at Arenenberg, they were encouraged to meet. The young Louis was a frequent visitor to Florence, and it was there that he became infected with his brother's passionate adolescent fervour for the causes of liberalism and Italian unity. In 1830 the two young men – Louis was just twenty-two – decided to abandon everything to join the ranks of the Carbonari at that moment committed to the revolt in the Romagna. Both saw action at Terni and at Civita Castellana, and both were unstintingly praised for their gallantry under fire.

The Carbonari leader, however, a Colonel Armandi, was

beginning to find the presence of two such famous young men more of an embarrassment than an asset. He had been hoping for help from France, which he felt was likely to be withheld when it became known that two members of the proscribed imperial family were serving in his ranks. The brothers were decorated for their bravery and then told in no uncertain terms that they must make their way home with the utmost speed.

During their dangerous exodus, dodging Austrian patrols actively searching for them, both succumbed to a measles epidemic. Napoleon Louis died. Louis might have shared his fate or at least have been captured by the Austrians but for a remarkable feat by Hortense, who, haunted by the fear that her two sons were in mortal danger, profited by her friendship with the British Minister in Tuscany to obtain a passport in the name of 'Mrs Hamilton and her two sons' and set off on a mad pilgrimage to track them down.

Leaving Foligno on 10 March, she spent several days on the road before eventually running Louis to earth at Pesaro. She found him desperately sick, barely strong enough to break the tragic news that Napoleon Louis was already dead. They managed to make their way to Ancona, where Louis collapsed. They were occupying a property that had belonged to Hortense's dead brother Eugène, where she hoped to be left in peace to nurse Louis back to health, but the day after they moved in, the Austrians arrived in the city. Showing a most admirable calm in the face of great danger, Hortense pretended to be ill herself, hiding Louis in her dressing-room. The Austrian colonel commandeered the building but was persuaded to allow 'Mrs Hamilton' to retain a few rooms for herself. While feigning convalescence, she was able to care for Louis and at the same time cunningly managed to spread rumours that someone answering to the wanted young prince's description had got away a few days previously to board a Corfu-bound boat.

When at last she pronounced herself fit to travel, she had also inveigled the unsuspecting Austrian officer into providing her and her footman, in actual fact Louis disguised in livery, with a *laissez-passer* through the Austrian lines.

From the time of their return to Arenenberg, Louis was too

busy (plotting to step into his uncle's shoes and spending considerable periods of his existence in either exile or gaol) to pay further attention to Italy and her problems. Even so, Victor Emmanuel could not rid himself of a deep-rooted conviction that Louis's old romantic enthusiasm for Italian independence must lie dormant, and was therefore determined to make the acquaintance of the one whom he saw as destined to be a powerful ally, at the earliest opportunity.

It was 1855 before the two men finally met, by which time Louis Napoleon had become Prince-President of France and then Emperor Napoleon III, and the Crimean War in which Piedmont was playing a minor role was entering its closing stage. The Crimean War brought about the first *rapprochement*. And from the King's point of view participation had been very much of a gamble.

Victor Emmanuel felt that all those domestic problems he had inherited had been happily resolved and essential internal peace within his domains firmly secured. The moment had arrived therefore, to build up the essential alliance, or alliances, abroad, a necessary prelude to the struggle to rid the peninsula of the Austrians. The possibility of war seemed to offer a heaven-sent opportunity for Piedmont to ingratiate herself with the two powers most likely to lend a sympathetic ear in the future struggle for which the country was now braced, namely France and Britain all the more so as there were indications that Austria was likely to remain neutral.

Cavour was more cautious. He feared that, with the bulk of her forces engaged in a war some two thousand miles from home, Piedmont would be dangerously exposed to any hostile move from her giant neighbour. Victor Emmanuel acknowledged the risk but felt that the political advantages of being officially allied to the two great western powers far outweighed the possible danger. If Piedmontese soldiers were fighting side by side with the British and French, he argued, the latter would feel honour-bound to protect Piedmont from any outside aggression.

When Parliament was informed of the proposed move, nearly every member showed himself to be bitterly hostile. The deputies, like Cavour, could only see the immediate risks involved rather than future advantages. Senior army officers were of the same way of thinking. For a moment it looked as though there might be a threat to the harmonious relations between the various political factions on which the King had been congratulating himself. In addition, the country was afflicted by a serious outbreak of cholera, while the lucrative trade which Genoa had established with Odessa had been halted by a blockade imposed on Russian shipping. Suddenly a recrudescence of left-wing agitation seemed possible. These internal crises, however, only made Victor Emmanuel, like many other a ruler both before and after him, the more determined to divert attention from domestic affairs by stirring up passions involving the current situation abroad.

Finally the King was able to persuade Cavour that, with so much at stake, there could be no question of hesitation. The Foreign Minister, Dabormida, was instructed to approach the British and French Ambassadors, Lord Hudson and the Duc de Gramont, to try to extract an official guarantee that, should Piedmont commit the bulk of her army to the Russian theatre of war, any attempted invasion of Piedmont by a third party would be considered a *casus belli* and that, when the war ended, 'the condition of Italy would be taken into consideration'.

Unfortunately there was still a possibility that Austria might be persuaded to abandon her policy of neutrality. The ambassadors, therefore, were unwilling to do more than give vague verbal assurances, even though, on the declaration of war on 27 March 1854 by France, Britain and Turkey, all western powers had been invited to join 'a nineteenth-century crusade against the barbarian Russians'.

Wrangling was still continuing when the allies landed in the Crimea. The battles of the Alma, Balaclava and Inkerman were fought, after which the Russians retired behind the shelter of Sebastopol's ramparts, leaving the besiegers to face a Russian winter in the open field.

The casualty lists published after the Crimean battles caused a wave of isolationism to sweep the British Isles. Lord Palmerston received a letter with the shrewd suggestion, 'Could we not engage some ready made and disciplined force? Might we not get six thousand men from Portugal, ten thousand men from Spain, and ten thousand from Piedmont to be taken on British pay, with their own officers, just as they are, but under the orders of our Commander-in-Chief?'

Lord Hudson was instructed to get the matter of Piedmontese participation settled and to urge the despatch of a contingent 'before the war ended'. He was certain that not only Austria but France also was hostile to the idea and said so in his communiqués. But though Austria had signed a 'convention' with the allies and actually mobilized a huge army, it was soon obvious that her activities would be theoretical rather than practical and that it was unlikely that a single Austrian soldier would leave his homeland. France did join her plea, even if somewhat hesitantly, to that of Britain. Finally, after shrewd bargaining on Cavour's part – he had in the meantime taken over from Dabormida – a treaty was signed on 10 January 1855 to the effect that Piedmont, in return for a British loan of half a million pounds, agreed to send an expeditionary force of fifteen thousand men to the Crimea.

Cavour then delivered an impassioned speech to Parliament which won the day by eighty-five votes to sixty-four. Piedmontese participation, he insisted, would result in 'a restoration of her (Piedmont's) reputation, so that all the peoples of the world, both rulers and ruled, may do justice to her qualities. And therefore two things are necessary; first to prove to Europe that Italy has political intelligence enough to conduct herself properly; secondly to prove to her neighbours that her military value is equal to that of her ancestors. And I am sure that the laurels which our soldiers will win in the regions of the East will do more for Italy's future than anything achieved by those who have believed that they were effecting her regeneration with voice and pen!'

It had been Victor Emmanuel's intention to give command to his brother, the Duke of Genoa, who had shown such courage at Novara, for, much as he would have preferred to have led his army himself, he felt the general situation was not settled enough to justify his absence at a distance of over two thousand miles from home. Sadly, just before the convoy was due to sail, the Duke died. Despite his doubts regarding the wisdom of the adventure, General La Marmora was persuaded to step into the Duke's shoes. He was to prove a sound, but far from inspired, leader. For the sake of Piedmont's military standing, it was indeed a pity that the King considered himself obliged to remain in his captial.

The allies, especially the French, displayed little confidence in the Piedmontese soldiers' battle potential. The war had degenerated into a static stage, but even so, initially La Marmora found himself relegated to a purely reserve role. His force played no part in the skirmishes which developed when the Russians made one of their many sorties, or when either the British or the French launched an attack on an enemy strongpoint. La Marmora was expressing the fear that disease – cholera raged – would destroy his army before it had had the time to prove its worth. Cavour and the King were worried by the thought that Russia might demand an armistice before the Piedmontese had fired a single shot.

However, on 11 August La Marmora was given his chance. On that day the Russians made a determined effort to smash the allied ring encircling Sebastopol by delivering a surprise assault, directed by General Gortchakoff in person, on the French and Piedmontese troops holding the line of the Tchernaya river valley. The brunt of the onslaught fell on the French, but one of La Marmora's brigades was heavily engaged. Though its losses were comparatively small – 188 killed and wounded as against 1,500 French and 8,000 Russians – the action provided just that sop to national pride and antidote to Novara for which Victor Emmanuel and most of his subjects had been praying, and which Cavour was quick to exploit to the full.

Sergeant-Major Gowing of the 7th Fusiliers mentions in his memoirs that, 'In the valley of the Tchernaya the enemy made a most determined attempt for victory, but the allies met them at all points and drove them back with terrific slaughter. I find that the Sardinians fought with desperation, well supported by the French ...' In his order of the day, Lieutenant-General Sir James Simpson wrote: 'The Sardinian army has shown itself worthy to fight by the side of the greatest military nations of Europe,' while the British Government sent an official note to

Turin after the fall of Sebastopol stating that the Piedmontese had 'gloriously contributed to the fall of Sebastopol by defeating the Russians on the Tchernaya and thereby contributing to the failure of the general attack which is now known to have been meditated by the Russians'. In fact a very good understanding seems to have been established between the British and the Piedmontese; one war correspondent gives this account of the return home of the armies after the armistice: 'The departure of General Della (*sic*) Marmora and his picturesque Sardinians was marked by many demonstrations of the regard and esteem in which our army held them. On the day they embarked, all our shipping hoisted the Sardinian flag; the yards of the *Leander* were manned, and the moment the General set his foot on her deck there rang from sea to shore three hearty English hurrahs ... they (the Sardinians) have left behind them many kindly remembrances not readily to be forgotten.'

'We repulsed the Russians to the cries of *Viva il Re! Viva la Patria!*' Cavour wrote to Madame La Marmora. And to the General himself: 'I cannot delay expressing to you the immense satisfaction with which the entire country has received the news conveyed by you in your telegraphic despatch in which you announce the brilliant feat of arms on the Tchernaya where for the first time our troops have had the chance of showing of what they are capable when fighting under a leader worthy to command them. The news has raised the spirit of the nation and reconciled everyone to the policy of the alliance.'

It is doubtful whether any battle, with the possible exception of Plassey, has ever gained such immense political advantages at so low a cost.

At home the King's popularity again soared. Perhaps even more important, he could now claim that he had 'arrived' internationally. Towards the end of the year, he paid state visits to both Britain and France, while Piedmont, represented by Cavour, took her seat at the international Congress called to work out peace terms in early 1856 in Paris.

During the British visit, Victor Emmanuel was on his best behaviour and did not, as Cavour feared he might, shock Queen Victoria and her staid consort by his overbluff manner and speech.

The Prime Minister's misgivings were well founded. Victor Emmanuel took a pride in being what was known as a 'man's man' in his titles of '*il re soldato*' and '*il re galantuomo*', the very reverse of his father, Charles Albert. Shortish, stockily built, he cultivated a genial air of extrovert *bonhomie*, which could, however, quickly change to blazing anger. His face was round, his jaw aggressive, his neck thick; at first sight one would have said a tough, ruthless, obviously successful big landowner. He gloried in this image – so much so that one may suspect that at times his notoriously unregal manner of speech, its perhaps deliberate coarseness, was an act, a playing to the gallery to enhance his reputation of plebeian monarch, an image he was at pains to encourage.

That he could assume a cloak of dignity at will was proved by his visit to Britain. A speech made during a banquet offered by the Lord Mayor of London was a great success in which he stated that 'the high place that England has attained' was due 'alike to the free and noble character of the nation and the virtues of your Queen'. In Paris, however, he did not seem to realize that such an approach was just as important to win favour with the ruler of the newly established Second Empire and his Empress. He imagined that Napoleon, who frequently, and with some bitterness, referred to himself as a '*parvenu*' monarch would appreciate a relaxation of protocol and the stifling formalities of normal Court circles. This indeed Napoleon might have done, but Victor Emmanuel's general behaviour aroused an intense antagonism on the part of the Empress Eugénie, who was not only a stickler for etiquette but a fanatical Catholic and, as such, an admirer of the Austrian Emperor as a pillar of the Faith while looking on Victor Emmanuel as the offspring of left-wing revolutionary trends menacing the pattern of life, to say nothing of the Pope's temporal power, which she herself would be prepared to defend with her life's blood.

If one story freely circulating at the time were true, it certainly did nothing to help the Piedmontese cause. On the occasion of an official reception at the Tuileries, Victor Emmanuel was asked what was his opinion of French women. '*Je me suis aperçu*' he was said to have replied, '*qu'elles ne portent pas des pantalons comme celles de Turin. C'est le paradis ouvert!'* ('I have noticed that, unlike the women of Turin, they do not wear drawers. It is an open paradise!')

Nevertheless despite Eugénie's disapproval of their royal guest, Napoleon had come round to the idea that an active alliance with Piedmont was not only inevitable but desirable, and on one occasion he managed to corner Cavour and ask quite openly what France could do for Piedmont. Though not by any means the war-monger that many of his detractors have made him out to be, he was haunted by the feeling that, if his dynasty were to endure and he were to be genuinely received into the exclusive club of reigning monarchs, he must further enhance his prestige. And by what better means than support of a cause which world opinion would deem to be the righting of a cruel wrong, such as that of Italian unity, where most were prepared to applaud but few, if any, to act?

Though on his return to Turin, Victor Emmanuel was congratulating himself that he had gained that personal friendship with the French ruler of which he had hinted in his post-Novara talks with Radetsky, he was deeply disappointed by Cavour's seeming failure to gain any benefits from the Paris Congress.

The Congress had to a certain extent been sponsored by Austria, anxious to see the end of the Crimean conflict. The armistice – the result of this intervention pressed after the fall of Sebastopol – had happened too soon, both Victor Emmanuel and Cavour had grumbled. The Piedmontese needed a second Tchernaya to establish themselves. Furthermore, the Congress brought Austria back into the international limelight – undeservedly so, since not a single Austrian casualty had been sustained.

During the debates, Cavour had been made to feel that he represented a very *minor* power and that, in the presence of the major powers, his attitude should above all be deferential, which was clearly meant to imply that it was not reasonable of him to imagine that anyone would risk giving offence to Austria to satisfy Piedmont's rather tiresome demands!

Most disappointing, perhaps, was Britain's negative behaviour. Napoleon had, for his part, made some effort to obtain control of Parma and Modena for his friend the King, but Austria would not hear of it, and as Cavour commented bitterly, 'The devil has it that the Empress (Eugénie) should desire the Pope to be godfather to her unborn child. This has gone far to wrecking my plans.'

But Cavour had not allowed himself to be intimidated, and his speech pleading for the recognition of Italy as such was recorded as one of the most impressive of the whole Congress. Piedmont was in a truly difficult position, he declared, for all around herself she saw 'in the rest of the peninsula, the peoples kept in a permanent condition of revolutionary disquiet by the reactionary and violent operations of bad governments ... herself threatened by Austria who had made a military occupation of a great part of the peninsula, and thereby destroying the balance of the various Italian states'.

Before leaving Paris, Cavour was able to hold private talks with both the Emperor and the British representative, Lord Clarendon, assuring them that the 'Italian question' could be resolved only by war. He was encouraged by discreet promises of support. From Paris he paid a quick visit to Britain. This proved to be a cruel deception. It was made amply clear to him that, though Britain was prepared to offer wholehearted moral support, not a single British soldier would be fighting alongside his erstwhile 'Sardinian' comrades, and not a single pound would be available to swell Piedmont's treasury. France was indeed the only hope.

'The case of Italy', said Cavour in his first speech to Parliament following on his return, 'is now before the bar of public opinion, before that tribunal which, in the memorable words of the French Emperor, must deliver its final verdict and proclaim the ultimate victory.'

Brave words. But the King's disgusted comment – 'Not even a duchy' – was a more apt summing-up of the whole Crimean adventure.

At this stage Cavour descended to a policy which smacked of the cheap novelette ...

The Prime Minister had an exceptionally beautiful, very young cousin, Virginia, Countess of Castiglione (née Oldoini), who did not suffer from modesty where her looks were concerned. '*Il Padre eterno non sapeva cosa si facero quel giorno che l'ha messa al mondo*,' she wrote of herself in old age, living, as a recluse, on the memories of her lost beauty. '*La impastata tanto e tanto e quando l'ha avuto fatta, ha perso la testa vedendo la sua maravigliosa opera*.' ('The Eternal Father did not realize what he had created the day he brought her into the world; he formed and reformed her so superbly that when it was done he lost his head at the contemplation of his marvellous work.') In all fairness, though, it must be added that most of her contempories shared her opinion.

Princess Metternich, wife of the last Austrian Ambassador to the Second Empire, described her as 'Venus come down from Olympus', admitting, 'I have never seen such beauty as hers and never will again.' Loliée says that 'she was one of those whom Saint Simon said were born to create *grands désordres d'amour*.' He went on: 'Shortly after the age of twelve she had her own box at the opera where her flashing eyes, promising figure and self assurance attracted everyone's attention. She became the idol of that pagan and artistic city, Florence.'

At the age of fifteen she met and married Count Francesco Verasis-Castiglione. The Count was soon aware that he had not been fortunate in his choice of a bride. Within two years he had dissipated his fortune in vain attempts to win her affection.

Her beauty and obvious dislike of her husband suited Cavour. Already, by late 1855, Virginia had been seduced, one might almost say raped, by Victor Emmanuel. The event was noted casually in the Countess's diary describing a garden party: 'I went for a stroll in the garden with the King. He ravished me. After that I went into the toilettes to tidy up.'

On hearing of this, Cavour decided to employ her in the role of a modern Delilah.

The Emperor Napoleon never troubled to hide the fact that he was 'tortured by the desires of the flesh'. Despite her totally undeserved reputation of loose-living, the Empress Eugénie was in fact verging on the prudish. Her dream of married life's fulfilment was achieved when the young Prince Imperial was born during the Congress of Paris. Her doctors had warned her that a second pregnancy might prove fatal, and as a result Napoleon was virtually expelled from her bed.

Virginia di Castiglione was therefore sent, quasi-officially, to Paris with formal instructions to become the Emperor's mistress and 'to do something for Italy'.

Whether or not she was able to influence Napoleon beyond the walls of the bedroom is an open question, but there can be no doubt that she was the first of a long line of imperial mistresses. She was in fact so delighted by her success that she confided in a friend, 'My mother was a fool. Instead of tying us up, Castiglione and me, she should have taken me to Paris a few years earlier, and it wouldn't have been a Spanish woman now installed in the Tuileries, but an Italian.'

Count Fleury, one of Napoleon's ADCs and a close personal friend, strenuously denies that La Castiglione had any influence on the Emperor's political life. 'She came to Paris with the *idée fixe* of seducing the Emperor,' he says in his memoirs, 'and of playing the role of supreme mistress. She succeeded in the first part of her programme but failed miserably where the second was concerned ... she soon wearied the man she hoped to ensnare and, after a year, dropped back into obscurity from which she never emerged.'

4

The Orsini Bomb

While Radetsky had been winning his decisive victories over Charles Albert, Austria, as has been seen, had not escaped the upheavals of 1848, when mob fury erupted obliging the imperial Court to flee to Vienna.

It was a flight which radically changed the course of Austrian history.

The old Emperor Francis I had been succeeded by Ferdinand, a man of great and gentle charm but generally considered a semi-imbecile, married but childless. This meant that the throne must eventually be assumed by the Archduke Francis Charles, Francis's second son, married to Sophie of Bavaria. It had been an unhappy marriage, and Sophie's one ambition was to witness the accession of her elder son, Franz, an ambition to which she devoted herself with such determination, such single-mindedness of purpose, that she became known as 'the only one man among all the "Highnesses" at Court'.

When the temporary exiles at Innsbruck, then at Olmutz, were planning their counter-attack to crush the revolutionaries and re-enter Vienna, it was generally agreed that Ferdinand was not the man to restore imperial authority. Ferdinand was only too happy to step down, whereupon Sophie saw her opportunity. Francis Charles was a man completely devoid of ambition. She had no difficulty in persuading him to abdicate – even before he had been named Emperor – in favour of his elder son. So it was that on 2 December the eighteen-year-old Franz, who added the name Josef for the occasion, was proclaimed as the Emperor Franz Josef I, in the Archbishop's Palace in Olmutz.

In November, Field Marshal Windischgraetz effectively crushed the Vienna rebels. The Court returned, with the new Emperor, in February of the following year, 1849.

Franz Josef had no reason to entertain friendly feelings towards either France or Piedmont, or towards their rulers. Brought up to look upon monarchy as a divine right in the most rigid school of absolutism, he regarded France as still embodying the spirit of the French Revolution, the worst abomination as far as he was concerned. Nor could he forget that the man whom the 1848 Paris revolution had swept to power was the nephew of the 'upstart' who in the early years of the century had not only humiliated Austria on the battlefield but twice occupied Vienna, forcing his grandfather to flee the city, and had installed himself in the summer Palace of Schönbrunn.

Though Italy, in the shape of the kingdom of Piedmont and Sardinia, was no real threat to the Austrian Empire, and its new king no outsider, it was nevertheless a thorn in the flesh. Basically the nightmare of 1848 had been sparked off by Italian risings, and in particular 'The Five Glorious Days', all of which had been encouraged by Piedmont, and with armed support in the case of Lombardy. Furthermore, Victor Emmanuel seemed to be proving a traitor to his class by tolerating a spirit of liberalism within his domains.

In character, also, Franz Josef was the very antithesis of both Napoleon III and Victor Emmanuel.

Piedmont's king and Napoleon, even after he had become France's emperor, prided themselves on their accessibility to their subjects and on the fact that royalty in no way affected their humanity, their understanding of human weaknesses. Victor Emmanuel liked nothing better than to crack a coarse joke with his soldiers, while the French Court boasted of the ability of both Emperor and Empress – and especially the Emperor – to mix freely with guests both on state occasions and at the purely private entertainments given on their country estates which formed such a feature of the Second Empire.

But from the very first days of his reign, Franz Josef made it clear that, as Emperor by Divine Right, as far as he was concerned the world could be divided into two categories: the

Emperor and the others. He would listen to opinions but would never tolerate 'advice'. Nor would he permit any argument once his mind had been made up. 'I command to be obeyed,' was one of his favourite sayings.

One taste he shared with his two neighbours: a passion for the military life – so much so that he was seldom seen out of uniform. Yet his ambitions and yearning for military glory fell far short of his capabilities.

In 1848, before his accession, he had been allowed to take part in the battle of Santa Lucia in a cavalry charge, much to Marshal Radetsky's alarm, enhanced by the fact that the young Prince showed himself to be brave to the point of recklessness. The old Marshal trembled at the thought of a Piedmontese sabre or bullet ending the life of a future emperor. Before Custozza, to his immense relief he had managed to get the disgruntled Franz recalled to Innsbruck. However, when it came to the study of the intricacies of strategy and battlefield tactics, Franz lost interest. He was more fascinated by what is commonly known as 'spit and polish'. To quote the words of his instructor, a Colonel Hauslab: 'Gifts of generalship he does not have, but he will make a reliable junior officer.'

His passion for the army, and his very genuine concern for the well-being of the men and their conditions of service, failed to win him affection. There was always about him a certain coldness, a lack of human warmth, of charisma, that vital apanage of all great captains. There was respect, even admiration, but no devotion. His appearances amongst his troops never provoked those unrestrained, utterly spontaneous outbursts of cheering such as often greeted both Napoleon and Victor Emmanuel.

Nor did he have the gift of choosing talented subordinates and ministers.

The early years of his life were overshadowed by men who could well be described as evil geniuses. This was particularly true in the case of Count Karl Ludwig Grunne, whom Sophie had appointed Master of the Household to become 'a combination of elder brother and knowledgeable valet who could only be depended on to do one thing consistently: produce the wrong solution to any given problem', and Count

Ferdinand Buol-Schauenstein, a professional diplomat of Swiss descent who was called upon to take over the post of Minister of Foreign Affairs on the death of Prince Felix Schwarzenberg in 1852.

The adverse comments applied to Count Grunne were even more true of Count Buol. From start to finish his ministry was a disaster. The very opposite of the traditional diplomat in manner, verging as he did on downright rudeness, his arrogance frequently earned him the personal enmity of his colleagues. Speaking of an interview with him in March 1852, Lord Malmesbury said heatedly, 'He behaved in the most coarse and insolent manner ... I at last asked him if he were accustomed to speak to English ministers in that style; because I must tell him at once that I would not bear with it.'

Though Franz Josef convinced himself that he was indeed an absolute monarch, uniquely responsible for the direction of his country's affairs, it was due to the behind-the-scenes bungling of this calamitous couple that Austria found herself so unpopular with her western neighbours at the time of the Crimean War.

The possibility of war placed Austria in a truly difficult position. In the fierce struggle for survival marking the opening years of Franz Josef's reign, the Austrian army had failed to repeat its success against the Piedmontese when faced with the Hungarian rebels led by Lajos Kossuth. Though led by such a distinguished soldier as Field Marshal Windischgraetz, the imperial forces were halted in their drive on Budapest, then defeated in a pitched battle. Windischgraetz was replaced by General Baron von Welden, who, however, was no more successful and was soon sending frantic appeals for reinforcements which, at that moment, were not available. Franz Josef thereupon despatched a call for help to Czar Nicholas I.

The Czar was delighted. Though he professed a great personal regard for the young Emperor, he had no wish to see Austria too powerful. It was a matter of satisfaction to feel that in the future Franz Josef would be beholden to Russia for the preservation of his throne. Added to this was the fact that the Hungarian army was being led by two Polish generals, and this being the case, a Hungarian victory might well lead to further uprisings against Russian rule in troublesome Poland.

A Russian expeditionary force of close on 200,000 men marched through Galicia under the command of General Count Paskiewicz, while Welden was replaced by the infinitely tougher General Haynau. In the face of such overwhelming force Kossuth fled to Turkey, naming a General Gyorgey as his successor, who promptly surrendered, not to the Austrians but to the Russians.

The Austrians were furious when the Czar refused to hand over Gyorgey for trial, but nevetheless Franz Josef felt that he was under a deep obligation to the Russians, even though he very much resented the Czar's patronizing attitude.

The sense of being patronized was aggravated when, as the Turkish questioning was becoming more critical, he received a letter from the Czar stating that he intended to claim a substantial share of the disintegrating – as he imagined – Ottoman Empire, ending, 'I do not know what you may decide, but whatever you do, if it should come to Turkey making war on you, you may be assured that it will be precisely as though Turkey declared war on me.'

Shortly afterwards Franz Josef was outraged and almost won over to the future allies' side when Russian troops marched into Moldavia. His immediate reaction was to send a senior army officer, Feldzeugmeister von Gyulai (who in 1859 would win such unfortunate renown for his abysmal direction of the Italian campaign), to St Petersburg, bearing a strong protest. Much to his surprise, the Count was most cordially welcomed. After being lavishly entertained, he was handed a letter from the Czar for his sovereign, which began, 'My dear young friend', and which enthused about 'the warm and close relationship so happily developed between us' before revealing Russia's future policy: 'My action is determined. I shall not deflect from it. As I said in my last letter, I shall not cross the Danube so long as the Turks do not attack me on the left bank. The loud talk of England and France alarms me as little as does the presence of their fleets in the Dardanelles, and will not prevent my insisting on the satisfaction owed me by the Turkish government.'

Franz Josef was not altogether happy about the letter's implications. In his opinion the collapse of Turkey could encourage the liberal tendencies in western Europe he so feared and hated. In his reply he warned, 'The intimate bond between us might be more or less shattered if indeed the disappearance of the Sultan's power gave birth to revolutionary cells aimed at the disruption of the European monarchical system.'

The Czar, desperately anxious to prevent Austria from falling into the enemy camp, paid a visit to Olmutz, scene of Franz Josef's accession, and a few days later there was a second meeting, this time in Warsaw, where the two rulers were joined by King Frederick William of Prussia. Trying blandishments and flattery the Czar used such rhetorical phrases as 'defending the cause of Christendom' and 'the infamy of France and England in fighting for the Crescent'. Nevertheless, he was not to be deterred by warnings from either of his two guests, and within a few days of the meeting breaking up, the Russian Government declared war on Turkey.

The western allies landed in the Crimea in September 1854. Austria then proceeded to alienate herself still further. It was inconceivable perhaps that she should have allied herself with Russia. She should, therefore, either have remained strictly neutral or wholeheartedly thrown in her lot with the allies. She did neither. She signed a 'convention' with the western powers, as has been seen, mobilized a huge army of 450,000 men at vast cost to an already shaky exchequer, then refused to send a single battalion or squadron to the battle front. Understandably, both Britain and France were furious, feeling that they had been hoodwinked, while the Russians were even more angry. Czar Nicholas died in 1855, but Russian anger and resentment at what was felt to be gross ingratitude after the way that their country had rushed to aid the Austrians after their SOS at the moment of the Hungarian crisis, was expressed in a letter by Nicholas's successor, Alexander II. He accused Franz Josef of contributing to his father's death by breaking his heart when, 'instead of finding in you a faithful friend and ally whom he loved as his own son, he saw you follow a path which brought you ever closer to our enemies.'

Austria duly took her seat at the Paris Congress, but her representative was cold-shouldered by those of all the combatants. Her only satisfaction was that Piedmont failed to gain any material reward for her efforts.

Disappointed though Victor Emmanuel and Cavour were when the Paris Congress finally broke up, Cavour could not forget that Napoleon had actually asked him 'What can I do for Italy?' It was understandable that Napoleon had to tread carefully to avoid the accusation that he had inherited his uncle's 'lust for conquest'; it was now also obvious that only with France's help could the King of Piedmont ever become the King of Italy. It helped that Austria had made herself so generally unpopular over the Crimea, and just as the war with Russia had been held up as a 'crusade', so it was hoped that in some way a war with Austria might be presented as a 'crusade', against the forces of reaction which would ensure Great Britain's moral sympathy and the active support of French bayonets.

Conversations were engaged, contacts made, vague feelers put out in Paris. An alliance with France, so the optimistic were thinking, might be just round the corner, when on 15 January 1858, it was learned that the previous evening, an attempt had been made to assassinate Napoleon and Eugénie as they were on their way to a benefit performance at the opera on behalf of a well-known singer named Massol, and that this attempt had been carried out by a group of Italians headed by a man named Felice Orsini.

Writing to her mother, the Empress Eugénie said:

Yesterday towards $7h\frac{1}{2}$ or 8 o'clock we were arriving at the peristyle of the Opera when there was an explosion which shook the carriage. The coachman, keeping his head, whipped up the horses. A second detonation and we felt the carriage breaking up under us. However we managed to advance another pace. We were almost at the foot of the steps when a third bomb killed one of the horses and further damaged the carriage. Suddenly both doors flew open and, on the Emperor's side, I saw an unknown figure. At that moment indeed I admit that I believed all was over and my thoughts turned to God. Fortunately it was one of the police. We stepped out into the middle of a group of men bleeding profusely ... to show you how much we owe to God's will, I must tell you that the Emperor and I were the only ones practically unharmed, he with a scratch on the tip of the nose, I with a tiny, scarcely perceptible, splinter in the white of the eye. There was a hole through the Emperor's hat, and our coach was riddled with fragments of iron bigger than bullets ...

It was in fact a near miracle that the imperial couple found themselves alive, for no fewer than 150 people had been killed or seriously injured.

All preparations for the attempted assassination had actually been made in Britain, where Count Felice Orsini, a fanatical republican, had been living in exile after escaping from an Austrian prison in Mantua in 1854. It was in Britain that he had collected his gang of fellow Italian exiles, that the plot had been hatched and the bombs to be used manufactured. Yet it was not so much against Britain that indignation was aroused as against Italy.

It is difficult to understand what really motivated Orsini and his fellow conspirators. They, and above all Orsini, were well aware where Napoleon's sympathies lay, of the fact that he had so nearly lost his life fighting for Italian unity with the insurgent Carbonari, and that he had repeatedly stressed the fact that he meant to 'do something for Italy to reward her for the rôle she played in the Crimea'. And indeed this senseless assassination attempt could well have done his country's cause irreparable harm.

Appalled when he heard the news, Victor Emmanuel waited with trepidation for the first reactions from Paris. They were not long in coming and seemed to confirm his worst fears, shared to a possibly greater extent by Cavour.

'I have only to raise a finger,' Napoleon wrote menacingly, 'and my army and the whole of France will march enchanted to whatever spot I point out as the home of the assassins.'

Cavour was in despair. The situation was saved, however, by a response typical of Victor Emmanuel. He was not the man to eat humble pie, no matter what the circumstances. Instead of finding excuses, as Cavour wished him to do, he ordered one of his ADCs, General della Rocca, to proceed immediately to

Paris. Della Rocca was to demand an audience with the Emperor and, acting as Victor Emmanuel's spokesman, to express his horror and disgust at the attempt, and to reiterate that friendship with France in the person of Napoleon was his principal and dearest wish. 'Nevertheless,' the King added, 'you must point out that one does not treat a faithful ally in such a way. I have never tolerated compulsion from anyone. My path is that of untarnished honour, and to this honour I hold myself responsible to none but God and my people.'

Like his famous uncle, Napoleon III was an intensely human man. Instead of taking umbrage at Victor Emmanuel's message, he was enchanted. 'Now that is what I call courage,' he said warmly to della Rocca. 'Your King is a brave man. I love his answer. Write to him at once. Assure him that, in case of war with Austria, I will come and fight beside my faithfull ally.'

The trial of Orsini and his fellow would-be killers also reacted in Piedmont's favour.

A letter from Orsini himself explaining exactly why he had committed his crime was published in *Le Moniteur*. In it he emphasized that he bore the Emperor no ill will personally and indeed had always nourished the conviction that a French alliance was the key to future Italian 'freedom'. But France's action in suppressing the Roman Republic had made him believe that the Emperor had changed his politics to become an instrument of absolutism and continued Italian 'slavery'. The letter ended with a plea to the Emperor to revert to his former pro-Italian bias and indeed march with Victor Emmanuel to drive the Austrians back over the Alps.

Orsini was a tall, good-looking man whom nature had endowed with the air and physique of a professional romantic. This was probably responsible for the most extraordinary consequence of the whole affair. During the conspirators' trial, Orsini's bearing, his fearless defence, which he conducted personally without the aid of an *avocat*, and the uninhibited expression of the motives guiding him, completely won over the Empress Eugénie and, though perhaps to a lesser extent, Napoleon. As the trial drew to its close, Eugénie became a fervent defender of the man who had so coldly plotted her death.

'What drove Orsini to attempt the assassination was the

exaltation of a selfless individual. He worships liberty just as he abominates those who hold his country in bondage,' she proclaimed to all and sundry. 'It was not the Emperor of France he wished to kill, but the Austrian Emperor's friend. He is a brave, proud man whom I admire.'

When, inevitably, Orsini was condemned to death, Eugénie made scene after scene with Napoleon. But there could be no question of a reprieve. Too many French men and women had been killed or seriously wounded when the bombs went off. Two of those who played a less prominent role in the plot and who had not actually handled the bombs, however, had the death sentence commuted to life imprisonment.

Orsini himself mounted the scaffold on the morning of 13 March. He showed no signs of fear. In a style worthy of the last act of a Verdi opera, he shouted, '*Viva l'Italia ... Viva la Francia*', before offering his neck to the guillotine's knife.

In the end, therefore, it could almost be claimed that the bombs of the Rue Pelletier had served to strengthen the prospective Franco-Piedmont alliance rather than destroying it, as, for a moment, had seemed possible.

Cavour was then able to continue with his task of reconciling all shades of Piedmontese opinion to the idea of close liaison with France, still resented by some liberal voices in Parliament. On 16 April he delivered a speech pointing out that the time of airy idealism was passed, that if the dreamed-of unity were ever to be attained, facts, however disagreeable they might be, must be faced. 'When we compare our forces with those of the Powers (Austria, France, Great Britain) to which just now I referred, we cannot regard our position as free from peril.' He went on to state that, though Piedmont had tried to solve her problems over the conference table, such problems were usually finally resolved 'on the battlefield and by the battalions and squadrons of the different Powers. Therefore,' he concluded, 'it can be seen that Fortune does not always favour the cause of rigorous justice since she still is, as in the time of Frederick the Great, the friend of the big battalions. When a nation is unable to put a large army in the field, it must seek to gain, in its need, the support of friends and allies.'

Spring seemed to witness the further tightening of the bonds binding France and Piedmont. Messages were passing frequently between Paris and Turin, giving the impression that a French declaration of war on Austria to coincide with that of Piedmont was no longer a question of 'if' but 'when' and 'how', while the pro-Piedmontese party in France was greatly strengthened by the active aid of a group of fanatically pro-Italy idealists, which included Dr Conneau, the imperial physician, and Madame Hortense Cornu, a childhood friend of the Emperor from Arenenberg days.

Britain had ceased to be the most sought-after ally.

As time passed, Victor Emmanuel became more and more disillusioned by the British post-Congress of Paris attitude and the fact that it was rumoured that France had been warned that Britain would consider it a hostile act if French troops were to cross the Alps to wage war by the side of Piedmont against Austria.

But in May even Napoleon showed that he was not altogether happy about the prospective hostilities, and Dr Conneau informed Cavour that, as a result of an interview with the Emperor, he had to stress that the *casus belli* must be 'adequate' and that France would not be able to see her way to lending active support if the war were seen to be of a *revolutionary* nature.

This sudden, unexpected tension lasted all through the late spring and early summer, only ending when, to their intense relief, the King and Cavour were informed that Napoleon would be visiting Plombières in the Vosges, where he was in the habit of 'taking the waters' every July, and that he would be delighted if the Prime Minister would care to join him there for 'talks of a strictly confidential nature'.

There was no valid reason why Cavour should not have undertaken the journey and attended the talks under his own name, but, as in Napoleon, there was something of the born conspirator in his nature. It was, therefore, incognito with a false passport that he arrived in Plombières on the evening of 19 July as Signor Giuseppe Benso, and, as if to maintain the illusion, he did not call on Napoleon, by then installed in the regal apartment of the Grand Hotel, till eleven o'clock the following morning.

Both 'conspirators' were amused and flattered by the skill with which the secrecy of their rendezvous had been maintained when, during the course of their initial conversation, Napoleon received a telegram from his Foreign Minister, Count Walewski, stating that it was reliably reported that Cavour had crossed the French frontier at Strasbourg, travelling incognito.

5

The Troubled Partnership

Once the two men were safely closeted and with no possible leakage of either their rendezvous or the purpose of their talks, Napoleon came straight to the point by saying that his mind was now firmly made up. To quote Cavour's letter to Victor Emmanuel written from Baden-Baden on 24 July: 'As soon as I entered the Emperor's study, he raised the question which was the object of my journey. He began by saying that he had decided to support Piedmont with all his power in a war against Austria, provided that the war was undertaken for a non-revolutionary end which could be justified in the eyes of French and European public opinion.'

In this Napoleon was simply repeating his provisos of the past few months, but at the same time making it understood that it was in Piedmont's interest that these conditions should be fulfilled, rather than quoting them as an excuse for evading an uncomfortable commitment.

There followed a long conversation in the course of which several potential provocations for a declaration of war were turned down by the Emperor as being too petty, including a protest aimed at the obvious Austrian endeavours to ignore rulings of the Paris Congress such as the continued occupation of the Romagna, and the strengthening of the key cities of the Quadrilateral's fortifications.

Cavour was temporarily baffled, for, as he admitted, there came the moment when he had no further suggestions to put forward. His embarrassment was relieved, however, when Napoleon hit on the idea of examining in detail the *status quo* of each one of the Italian states, hoping thereby to find the solution to their problem.

King Victor Emmanuel of Piedmont, later the first king of Italy and (*inset*) Count Camillo Benso di Cavour, Victor Emmanuel's Prime Minister and one of the principal architects of the Unification of Italy.

(*Left*) The Austrian Emperor Franz Josef, reigned 1848–1916.

(*Below*) Field Marshal Josef Radetsky: victor of Custozza and Novara when 82 years of age. He died in 1858 before Italy's renewal of war with Austria.

GRAF RADETZKY
k.k. Ostr. Feldmarschall.

Napoleon III, Emperor of the French, reigned 1852–70.

(*inset*) **Prince Jerome Bonaparte, better known as 'Plon-Plon', cousin of the Emperor Napoleon III. He married Victor Emmanuel's daughter Clothilde to cement the Franco–Piedmontese alliance.**

(*Above*) A scene from the battle of Montebello (20 May 1859) when 6,000 French and Piedmontese commanded by General Forey defeated 15,000 Austrians.

(*Above right*) Lieutenant-General Morozzo della Rocca, chief of the Italian Army General Staff during the 1859 campaign.

(*Below*) The battle of Palestro, another allied victory. It was after this battle that the phrase *La furia francese* was coined.

(*Below right*) General Manfredo Fanti, commander of the 2nd Piedmontese Division at Solferino.

(*Above*) The Italian patriot and freedom fighter, Giuseppe Garibaldi, promoted to General by Victor Emmanuel.

(*Right*) General Alfonso La Marmora who commanded the Piedmontese contingent in the Crimea.

(*Below*) General Enrico Cialdini who commanded the Piedmontese contingent at Palestro and the 4th Division at Solferino.

The battle of Solferino (often referred to in Italy as San Martino). The attack on the *Mont des Cyprées*.

Colonel de Chabrière, killed as he lead a charge of the 2nd Foreign Legion infantry regiment at the battle of Magenta.

The charge of the *Chasseurs d'Afrique* at Solferino.

An Austrian view of the battle of Solferino.

(*Above*) The Emperor Napoleon III with his staff observing the final stages of the battle of Solferino.

(*Below left*) The Austrian Marshal, Prince Alexander von Hesse, rallies his men during a stage of the battle of Solferino.

(*Below right*) Field Marshal von Benedek, the only Austrian commander to show any evidence of military genius throughout the 1859 campaign.

At last – again according to Cavour, 'After we had gone over the whole peninsula without success, we arrived at Massa and Carrara, and there we discovered what we had been so ardently seeking. After I had given the Emperor a description of that unhappy country, of which he already had a clear enough idea, we agreed that we should persuade the inhabitants to petition Your Majesty, asking protection and even demanding the annexation of the duchies to Piedmont. This Your Majesty would decline, but you would take note of the Duke of Modena's oppressive policy and would address him a haughty and menacing note. The Duke, confident of Austrian support, would reply impertinently. Thereupon Your Majesty would occupy Massa and the war would begin.'

This twist, so Cavour argued, would, according to Napoleon, be certain to make it seem that the Duke was the guilty party and deliberately starting hostilities. Furthermore, as the Duke was considered generally as a pillar of despotism, sympathy, if not actual material aid, would be forthcoming from Britain and, in view of the bad blood still existing between Austria and Russia, ensure the latter's neutrality.

The practical Napoleon then insisted on discussing what exactly would be the 'objectives' of the war they were plotting. It was obvious that its principal aim was the chasing of the Austrian presence and influence once and for all from Italian soil 'without an inch of territory south of the Alps or west of the Isonzo'. That, however, still left a major problem as to the composition of the future Italian state.

At this stage, though clamouring for a united Italy, even Victor Emmanuel did not envisage the entire peninsula from the Alps to the toe of Italy, let alone Sicily, as a single nation under the green, red and white tricolor, but rather a kingdom of upper Italy which would be formed by the northern stretch, the valley of the Po and the Romagna, and a kingdom of central Italy. Rome would remain in the hands of the Pope, and the kingdom of Naples would retain its existing boundaries. It was hoped, however, that these four states might be persuaded to form a federation – based on that of Germany – a hope shared by Napoleon. Suggestions were also made as to who should be the ruler of this theoretical central kingdom – with its capital in Florence – and of Naples, where Napoleon was entertaining the secret hope that a member of the Murat family might be installed.

Napoleon then wished to know 'what would be in it for France' and proposed that Piedmont should cede Savoy and Nice. Cavour replied that he was inclined to agree to hand over Savoy but that 'by origin, language and custom, the people of Nice were closer to Piedmont than France, and consequently their incorporation into the Empire would be contrary to the very principle for which we are taking up arms. The Emperor' Cavour continued, 'stroked his moustache, and merely remarked that these were for him quite secondary questions which we could discuss later.'

The next matter on the agenda was 'how' the war could be won.

This discussion was based not so much on strategical as on political problems, for though Napoleon was far from considering that his uncle's military genius had been reborn in him, he undoubtedly felt an atavistic yearning to lead his army in just one successful campaign; Cavour, for his part, was wise enough to know his own limitations where matters military were concerned and always avoided interfering in the military sphere.

Both men agreed that, when it did come to the actual fighting, Austria must fight alone. There must be no possible excuse for anyone to enter the war on her side. Britain, in particular, must be kept neutral, and for that very reason, Napoleon stressed, he was planning a second meeting with Queen Victoria and her consort. It was fortunate also that Austria and Prussia were on far from friendly terms with each other, and that a renewed *entente* between France and Russia should effectively remove any threat from the Czar.

Nevertheless Napoleon did not under-estimate the dangers of the struggle that lay ahead. One thing ever-present in his mind was Austrian resilience. Time after time the Austrians had been defeated by his uncle, but in spite of terrible losses and the occupation of their capital on two occasions by the French army, they were never crushed. 'Austria', he said, 'was always back on the battlefield, ready to fight.' And he reminded

Cavour that 'in the last wars of the Empire, at the terrible battle of Leipzig, it was the Austrian battalions which contributed most to the defeat of France.' In fact he doubted whether victories in Italy would be enough to bring the war to a close, but rather foresaw the necessity of pushing on into the heart of Austria, even as far as the gates of Vienna, before Franz Josef would be prepared to sit at a conference table to discuss a peace based on satisfactory terms from the Italian point of view. All this meant full mobilization and the full commitment of the armed forces of both countries – at a rough estimate, 200,000 Frenchmen and 100,000 Piedmontese.

At this stage a unified command was not considered, but rather the formation of two armies, each with its monarch at its head. On the all-important matter of finance, Napoleon agreed that France would be prepared to act as Piedmont's arsenal and offer facilities for a suitable war loan.

With so much and such essential details satisfactorily arranged, it seems strange that so very unwarlike a matter as a marriage should risk causing the breakdown of the future alliance. Yet after all the major problems appeared to have been smoothed out, Cavour suddenly felt that all his work might well prove to have been in vain.

The exhaustive talks ended at about three o'clock in the afternoon. Napoleon then suggested that an hour later, after a well-earned rest and relaxation, Cavour should accompany him for a drive in the country.

The carriage, a phaeton, was drawn by American horses, and Napoleon took the reins. Only one servant accompanied them. They drove for a good three hours through the beautiful valleys and forests of the Vosges, during which time the conversation hinged entirely on the Emperor's request that his cousin Prince (Jerome) Napoleon – better known as 'Plon-Plon' – son of the youngest of the imperial Bonaparte family, Jerome, ex-King of Westphalia, should be given the hand in marriage of Victor Emmanuel's sixteen-year-old daughter, Clothilde.

In the past, Napoleon had thrown out hints as to the desirability of this marriage, but till then Victor Emmanuel had always managed to prevaricate, for the simple reason that the mere contemplation of such a 'union' appalled him. Though himself no prude, he strongly disapproved of 'Plon-Plon's mode of life. The Prince had the reputation of being totally amoral and an atheist. He was twenty years older than his prospective bride and looked considerably more. He was unhealthily stout, generally repellent physically. Even his own sister Mathilde, very much a 'woman of the world', had been heard to protest: *'Mais Jérôme chez Clothilde! C'est le Diable dans un bénitier!'* 'What, Jerome marry Clothilde! It would be like the Devil in a font!''

Cavour knew of the King's repugnance to the marriage and that, being a widower, he felt fiercely protective. He did his best to stall, but on this matter Napoleon was unusually obdurate. He hinted, and forcefully, that basically it was a question of 'no wedding, no French soldiers'. This Cavour pointed out in a letter to Victor Emmanuel, trying to convince him, at the same time, that 'Plon-Plon' was far from being as black as he was painted. 'Prince Napoleon,' he wrote, 'is much better than his reputation would have him to be. He is a *frondeur*. He loves to be contrary. But he is witty as well as sensible, and is warmhearted.'

For the sake of his country Victor Emmanuel felt obliged to force his daughter to play the role of a modern Iphigenia. Clothilde was duly despatched to Paris with a letter to Eugénie begging her to take the young bride under her wing 'for, poor child, she is very young and has need of a sister so kind to help her with advice. She is like a partridge, and has no ambition but to be nice to you.'

There is little doubt that Victor Emmanuel felt he had been blackmailed and could not forgive. From then on the personal friendship which should have existed between the two men, and which could well have ensured that the victories which were to come would have been all the more complete, simply did not exist. This was all the more sad in that Clothilde had no need of a protective wing. She was so enveloped in the armour of her piety as to be perfectly self-sufficient, and at the same time seemed to be endowed with a sullen superiority complex. When Eugénie, trying to be kind, said, 'You will soon be accustomed to my Court, dear,' Clothilde replied coldly, 'Oh, yes – I've been accustomed all my life to my father's.'

In spite of this one cloud, Cavour was of the opinion that his mission had succeeded fully, and it was buoyed up by a feeling of sublime optimism, that, before returning to Turin, he undertook a rapid tour to contact possible additional friends, visiting the King of Württemberg, the Grand Duchess Elena of Russia, the Crown Prince of Prussia and a high-ranking Russian diplomat named Balan. Writing to General La Marmora, he stressed: 'If one can rely on what was said to me by the Grand Duchess Elena and Balan, we can depend for certain on the armed support of Russia. Balan indeed assured me that "if you have a *chasseur de Vincennes* on one side of you, you can count on having a soldier of our Guard on the other".'

If a tiny shadow did exist, it was that the complete accord with the French Emperor was verbal. As A.J. Whyte says in his *Political Life of Cavour*, 'The essence of the task which lay before him was in the accomplishment of two things; to turn the pact made at Plombières into a signed treaty; and secondly to find an adequate *casus belli* that would justify Napoleon in fulfilling his share of the bargain.'

Faced by the prospect of an anti-Austrian coalition, Franz Josef decided to try to charm his unwilling, rebellious Italian subjects, hoping thereby to make foreign rule not only bearable but preferable to the troubled, austere régimes of the other states of the peninsula. Determined efforts were made to raise the general standard of living. Taxes were so drastically reduced that, materially, the people of Lombardy and Venetia found themselves better off than any of their neighbours. Corrupt Austrian officials were summarily dismissed. But it was too late. By then nationalist passions allied to a mounting xenophobia had reached such a pitch that Italians could no longer be wooed, as Franz Josef was forced to realize after the dismal failure of a 'good will' visit to Milan accompanied by his beautiful young wife, the Empress Elizabeth.

When the imperial carriage drove through the city, instead of the cheering crowds expected, an eerie silence prevailed. Pavements and balconies were deserted. No faces appeared at the windows. The memory of 'The Five Glorious Days' still remained vivid in the memories and minds of the Milanese, irrespective of rank or social status. This demonstration of dumb hostility was followed by a supreme rebuff on the night of a gala performance at the opera. The great families accepted the official invitations addressed to them but on the night itself sent their servants to occupy their stalls and boxes.

This should have proved beyond all shadow of doubt that a policy of reconciliation stood no chance of success, but Franz Josef was obstinate to the point of sheer stupidity. On returning to Vienna, he sent his younger brother, Maximilian, to Milan in the role of both Viceroy and Commander-in-Chief, after Radetsky had been prevailed upon to offer his retirement.

Maximilian was the European Prince Charming of the moment, swathed in an aura of romance. Popular rumour had it that his father was in fact the son of Napoleon I and his second wife, Marie Louise of Austria, known to history as '*l'Aiglon*', held in velvet captivity in Vienna after the fall of the First Empire till his death at the age of twenty-one from galloping consumption in 1832. But the Italians were not impressed. For them Maximilian was simply another detested foreigner.

The move, however, was more than just a political failure. Radetsky's retirement from the scene constituted a military disaster, for with the departure of the aged Field Marshal, that lurking inferiority complex felt by the Piedmontese, when measured against the Austrians, disappeared. In addition, as will be seen, Radetsky's successor, *Feldzeugmeister* Count Gyulai, one of the most inept of leaders ever to be given an active command, was largely to blame for the fatal errors of the early stages of hostilities which, the following year, would so largely contribute to the Franco-Piedmontese victory.

Obliged to recognize the fact that he could never win the affection of the Italians, who had made it all too evident that they would prefer to be misruled by an Italian than be members of a model society run by foreigners, Franz Josef did set about attempting to improve the army's general efficiency. Yet without Radetsky there was no one to judge whether proposed measures were likely to be effective and improve the battle potential of the vast mass of men under arms. Though Franz Josef, as has been seen, did not lack courage when under fire, he showed no gift for, and in fact little interest in, the finer points of military art. Because of his love of outward show, his ideas limited themselves to the planning of still more gorgeous uniforms and still more spectacular parades.

On paper the Austrian army was an awe-inspiring weapon of war, 800,000 strong, but it was grotesquely unwieldy and, it must again be emphasized, with one exception since Radetsky's retirement, incredibly amateurishly led. This one exception was Field Marshal Count Benedek, who, many have claimed, although on the losing side, was the only commander with any spark of genius on the field of Solferino. Unfortunately for Austria, Franz Josef's chronic inability to pick suitable men for the job in hand was again manifest. He never appreciated Benedek's talent; he did not even like him as a man; and yet nobody could have been a greater patriot or more loyal and devoted subject.

The army hierarchy was almost medieval. Even on active service most regiments were commanded by 'honorary' colonels who had spent little, if any, time with their units other than on the many ceremonial parades. Administration and training were left entirely in the hands of junior career officers who were disgracefully underpaid and had very little prestige and, because of so-called inferior birth, little or no hope of promotion to a senior rank. Units still manoeuvred in battle drill formations dating back to pre-Napoleonic days despite the significant increase of fire power. Administration was abominably inefficient, almost non-existent, as were medical services. Class distinction reached ridiculous proportions, affecting the various arms and precluding liaison in the field without which victory is impossible; the cavalry was aristocratic, gunners and sappers middle class, the infantry plebeian.

Another problem crippling the proper exercise of command was the fact that most of the army was made up of a polyglot mass of men of peasant origin, most of them – and many of the NCOs – illiterate, drawn from no fewer than ten linguistic groups, yet even in the despised infantry ninety per cent of the officers were German-speaking. The one asset which, time after time, overcame these seemingly insuperable difficulties was the undoubted bravery of these same ill-led men under fire, their stoicism and fortitude in putting up with the most appalling conditions and physical discomfort, and the unexpected – one might almost say, illogical – high morale which the wearing of their uniform instilled in them. Napoleon was right not to under-estimate his future opponent. With a more professional, intelligent commander – Benedek, for instance – on the outbreak of war, it is possible that the names of Magenta and Soferino would not be adorning two of the main Paris boulevards to recall past victories. Austria's major misfortune was that she so seldom produced a general of any real talent to lead such willing soldiers into battle, so that, time after time, her army became 'the gallant losers'. France, on the contrary, has throughout her history been able to honour many a 'great captain', a number of whom in the post-Napoleonic era learned their trade in French North Africa. It was more than unfortunate that this traditional line should twice be broken when the nation was in deadly peril, namely in 1870 and again in 1940.

Even as late as 1859, the French army, still basking in memories of 'la gloire', was considered to be the most powerful fighting force in Europe – before Prussian professionalism confounded the world by setting a new and altogether higher standard of thoroughness and machine-like efficiency in the waging of war. One great and unique advantage enjoyed by France in the 1859 campaign was that the metropolitan formations could be substantially, and in a comparatively short space of time, reinforced by units from the battle-tried army in Algeria. It was true that British and 'native' units had been fighting for over a century in India, thus gaining practical experience of battle conditions, but in the mid-nineteenth century this would have been of no advantage to Britain in a European campaign because of the interminable sailing time for a troopship from Bombay or Karachi before the opening of the Suez Canal. Only a few days at sea, however, enabled MacMahon's Africa Corps (which included such famous regiments as the Foreign Legion, Zouaves, *Chasseurs d'Afrique* and *Tirailleurs*) to reach Genoa, there to disembark and play such an outstanding role in the ensuing campaign as to arouse considerable resentment and jealousy on the part of such darlings of the French public as the Imperial Guard.

French officers of all grades, from *sous-lieutenant* to *maréchal*, were deeply aware of the vital importance of establishing a firm basis of trust and confidence with the rank and file, rather than being unable, even unwilling, to communicate with them. From company to army commander, French officers made a habit of sharing campaign hardships, scorning privilege and referring to their men – and thinking of them – as '*mes enfants*'; speaking to the men individually, the officers employed the familiar, paternal, second-person singular '*tu*'.

Undoubtedly the weakest of the three armies flexing its muscles before the threatened combat was that of Piedmont, a fact which Victor Emmanuel realized only too well since it had forced on him the not altogether happy alliance when he would have preferred to act independently, for, as well as never being able to forgive Napoleon for what amounted to a form of shotgun wedding, he was not altogether sure that he could trust him. As with the Austrian army, the great weakness of the Piedmontese lay in the senior officers. Despite the experience gained by all divisional commanders in the 1848 and '49 campaigns, not one of them seems to have learned from their mistakes or to have been spurred to endeavour to improve his handling of a tactical situation. This applied even to La Marmora, hero of the Tchernaya. Instead, each allowed himself to be motivated by excessive jealousy of his imagined rival rather than a desire to contribute to his country's victory, a tragic state of affairs which not even Victor Emmanuel was able to recify.

In the meantime, Napoleon was showing no signs of being in a hurry to commit the Plombières agreement to paper, thus making it binding. Instead, he requested the despatch of a 'confidential agent' in order to hold further discussions in Paris. The man chosen was Count Constantino Nigra, Cavour's private secretary. The first interview granted to Nigra by the Emperor in no way abated Victor Emmanuel's sneaking doubts as to his ally's sincerity, for Napoleon did not show himself to be in the friendliest of moods when he stated immediately that he was having second thoughts regarding the manoeuvre he and Cavour had worked out to make unrest in Massa-Carrara serve as the essential *casus belli*. In addition, Nigra was told categorically that the actual declaration of war would have to be delayed. Victor Emmanuel was counting on the spring of 1859. He realized this, said Napoleon, but he did not feel that he could be 'ready' by that date. The spring of 1860 would be preferable, or, at the *very earliest*, the late summer of 1859.

Cavour was as depressed as the King, fearing, understandably, that the Emperor now regretted his bargain and was 'cooling off'. Yet there was nothing that could be done other than exercise tact and patience, combined with discreet pleas. When it came to prolonged arguments, diplomatic haggling, Victor Emmanuel preferred to leave matters in the hands of his Prime Minister. Cavour saw fit, therefore, to beg Nigra to try to persuade Napoleon that undue delay might prove fatal. Though Austria was not popular on the international scene, the mood of diplomatic opinion was fickle and, he warned, could change overnight. There was always the possibility that Austria's apparent 'peace at any price' approach, which Cavour suspected was merely a blind, might begin to take effect.

Hopes soared when Nigra was able to report that not only did Napoleon find that the arguments put to him made sense, but there was also further encouraging news of Russia's probable attitude in the case of a conflict. The Czar, apparently, still bore Franz Josef a personal grudge for his behaviour at the time of the Crimea and had let it be known that, provided Britain could be persuaded to remain strictly neutral, he might well be prepared to back the Franco-Piedmontese with both ships and a contingent of considerable strength. Napoleon also mentioned to Nigra that he was getting a little impatient that arrangements for the royal wedding seemed to be hanging fire, and that he would appreciate news of the arrival of the bride-to-be in Paris in the not too distant future. This being the case, General Niel, one of the most distinguished of French commanders who had won a great reputation for himself before Sebastopol, would be visiting

Turin with full powers to act for the French Government, bringing with him for signature a public and a secret treaty, a military and financial convention and official documents concerning the marriage.

It appeared that the last difficulties had been cleared up. Optimism, however, was soon banished when the actual text of the documents Niel would be bearing was disclosed to Nigra – understandably so, for many of the main points of the Plombières agreement had been either eliminated, radically modified or even changed in a contrary sense.

At Plombières it was Napoleon who had suggested a joint command and who had promised to facilitate a loan for the vast expenses war must inevitably incur. But article 5 of the secret treaty stated: 'The cost of war will be born by the Kingdom of Upper Italy (Piedmont)', a rider adding: 'All expenses of the war will be reimbursed to France by annual payments of one tenth of all revenues of Upper Italy.'

In the military convention, it was specified that supreme command of the allied army should be invested in Napoleon. This army was to be split into two sectors with the French and forty thousand Piedmontese, under General La Marmora, operating on the left bank of the Po, the remainder of the Piedmontese under the King on the right bank. The convention also laid down that Genoa, which would be the port of disembarkation for most of the French army, would, for the duration of the war, be under a French military governor to be nominated by the Emperor.

To gain time to think up counter-suggestions, Cavour was ordered to write immediately to Nigra to say that such vital amendments to the original plan could not be discussed satisfactorily with General Niel, and that the documents should be presented by someone of no less standing than 'Plon-Plon' himself. Matters thus remained in temporary abeyance, but further difficulties arose when Napoleon felt obliged to inform his Foreign Minister, Count Walewski, that he was planning to help the Piedmontese chase the Austrians from the Italian peninsula, by force of arms if necessary.

Walewski was known to be fanatically pro-Austrian and to entertain a hearty dislike of both Victor Emmanuel and

Cavour. Later Napoleon told Nigra: 'I could have wished for a year before venturing on our plans, but I have decided to hasten the moment of action to fit in with your plans.'

Something of a diplomatic shuttlecock, Nigra hurried back to Turin, stayed a few days and then was once more back in Paris in time for Christmas and with an invitation to 'Plon-Plon' to visit Turin the following month, January 1859.

It was, however, an anxious ending to a year which had promised so much for Piedmont's hopes. For not only was Napoleon appearing to hedge, but for some inexplicable reason even British moral support seemed to be melting away, and although the Italians had shown little or no response to Austrian overtures, as Cavour pointed out in a letter to the French Emperor, the Archduke Maximilian was 'making the greatest efforts to win popularity with his pomp and ceremony, with largesse, brilliant shows and free festivals'. He went on: 'Of course the chosen few will resist, but I am very doubtful about the masses ... the King begs Your Majesty to weigh up with your great wisdom these political and military considerations and he hopes we can agree to start hostilities if not in April, at least by July 1859.'

Victor Emmanuel, for all his worries, remained remarkably calm. Possibly he had a sense of destiny, a certitude that, right being on his side, he would triumph in the end, overcoming the many obstacles that now loomed up to block his path. Cavour on the other hand was becoming frantic, feeling that time was a matter of the utmost importance since every passing day served only to weaken Napoleon's resolve. Like the proverbial drowning man, he was clutching at straws, seeking to discover and exploit any trend which might lead to Austria's embarrassment. In December he endeavoured to open negotiations with a possible Hungarian dissident, General Klapka. He also despatched a secret agent to Belgrade on hearing that the Serbs were in a belligerent mood.

'Wishful thinking' became manifest on his part. When Odo Russell, British representative in Rome, stopped in Turin *en route* for the Eternal City, Cavour assured him that it would be 'an interesting winter' as there would be war with Austria. Russell was blunt. He repeated the official line that Britain intended to adopt, namely that if Piedmont deliberately provoked a conflict, she would be boycotted by the rest of Europe. Cavour replied confidently that he understood perfectly but that the aggressor would be Austria. In answer to Russell's frankly expressed doubts, he stated, with an assurance he was probably far from feeling, that he would 'force her to declare war on us'.

6
The Clouds Burst

Every year, on new year's day, Napoleon held a reception for the diplomatic corps. It was a conventional ceremony, never varying from year to year. As the doyen of the corps, the Papal Nuncio would address a message of good will to the Emperor, who would then exchange a few friendly words with each member present. On this occasion, 1 January 1859, when Napoleon came to speak with Baron Hubner, the Austrian Ambassador, he eyed him in silence for a moment, then said in icy tones, 'I regret that my relations with Austria are not as good as I could wish, but I beg you will write to Vienna that my personal sentiments towards the Emperor remain the same.'

It was a dramatic start to the year.

The fact that war appeared to be in the air created a panic in financial circles. Shares sank to an all-time low on the stock markets of Europe, the alarm not allayed by a leading official of the British Embassy in Paris who publicly announced that it would not be long before the first shots were fired, or by Victor Emmanuel who, in his opening of Parliament speech on 18 January, asserted that Piedmont, small country that she was, could not 'rest insensible to the *grido di dolore* (cry of grief) that reaches us from so many parts of Italy'.

The question of Italy's future was now the principal problem facing European diplomacy, and one from which none of the major powers felt that they could stand aloof.

Britain preferred that the *status quo* should not be unduly disturbed, always haunted by the fear that a resounding Franco-Piedmontese victory might leave France too strong. Negotiations aimed at preventing war were handled by Lord

Malmesbury, who objected to the term '*grido di dolore*' in Victor Emmanuel's speech whereby 'the head of a Government, unassailed by any foreign power, and with no point of honour at stake, appears to invite a European war by addressing himself to the suffering subjects of other powers'. Prussia strongly criticized Napoleon's snub to Baron Hubner. The Russians let it be known that they were preparing a 'peace plan' and did not expect any 'action' till this had been duly presented for study. Austria reacted by sending an army corps, the 3rd, to Lombardy when Count Buol evinced the opinion that 'possible changes in Italy endanger the basic treaties of 1815 which have effectively preserved general peace in Europe since that date'. This statement, palpably untrue in view of the 1848 and 1849 campaigns and the Crimean War, was nevertheless echoed and much quoted by Lord Malmesbury.

The marriage between 'Plon-Plon' and Princess Clothilde was duly celebrated at the end of January. Napoleon, therefore, no longer had any basic excuse for not pushing on with plans to honour the Plombières agreement, especially as, in addition, the original objections to the cession of Nice, once victory had been achieved, had been waived. But mounting European hostility to the now obvious conspiracy between France and Piedmont to bring about war was compelling the Emperor to entertain second thoughts; above all he feared Britain's reaction once a French expeditionary force landed on Italian soil, since the anti-war lobby in Westminster was becoming stronger daily. Nor could he count on the whole-hearted support of his own people. The hostility to the project openly shown by the Foreign Minister, Count Walewski, was particularly worrying, and the behind-the-scenes influence of the Empress Eugénie (more than ever convinced that Austria stood for established law and order and the upholding of the Faith, whereas the Piedmont of Victor Emmanuel represented the powers of darkness, anarchy and heresy) was beginning to fray his nerves.

At the beginning of February, Napoleon had felt obliged to write to Victor Emmanuel warning of Britain's 'negative' attitude and the danger that Prussia, who 'out of jealousy of France shows herself very badly disposed towards Italy', might actually fight on the Austrian side. As a result of these unexpected reactions throughout Europe, Napoleon went on to say that he advised Piedmont 'to prepare *slowly* for war ... to arm and strengthen the fortresses, to accumulate munitions and provisions'. He went on to warn that it was going to be exceedingly difficult to 'provoke' Austria – as Cavour had promised Odo Russell – since she will do everything possible to escape war'.

As if to confirm Napoleon's forebodings, Victor Emmanuel received an official communiqué a few days later from Lord Malmesbury, accusing Piedmont of belligerency and requesting a 'detailed statement of Italian grievances'. Malmesbury duly received his requested detailed reply but was evidently not impressed. At the same time further pressure was being brought to bear on France not to interfere in any Austro-Piedmontese wrangle.

Napoleon was in despair. He was not the sort of man to renounce a pledge given in all good faith. And as Piedmont's baffled anger increased, and angry communications winged their way between Paris and Turin, he felt obliged to make a public and official reply as to his exact position in the bitter dispute between two supposed allies. In early March *Le Moniteur* published a communiqué to the effect that, 'The Emperor has promised the King of Sardinia to defend him against every aggressive act of Austria; *he has promised nothing more and will keep his word.*'

The following day Count Buol granted an audience to Lord Cowley, who had gone to Vienna as Lord Malmesbury's representative, vigorously denying that Austria entertained hostile feelings or harboured hostile intentions *vis-à-vis* Piedmont. But no sooner had this conciliatory statement been made than it was learned that another Austrian corps, the 2nd was *en route* for Lombardy. Piedmont's reply was to order partial mobilization and to enrol into the ranks over two thousand Italians, political refugees from foreign rule.

Russia now stepped in with a plan that a congress be called to settle the vexed question, a move resented by Britain, who till then felt that London's was the voice dominating the complicated drama. Cavour was totally opposed to the idea, remarking that, whenever a congress had been held in the past Piedmont always emerged as the one party to be the overall loser. Napoleon, however, was adamant that the Russian plan should go ahead, seeing thereby a possible way of avoiding, with honour, his commitments. The whole of Piedmont was then shocked and appalled when it was announced that the congress was to be limited to representatives of the five major powers: France, Britain, Russia, Prussia and Austria. In addition this shattering information was accompanied by a bald statement more or less ordering Piedmont to disarm.

These distressing developments had a grave effect on Victor Emmanuel's till then exemplary courage. Apart from the bitter frustration of seeing such well-founded hopes collapsing, he felt all the more keenly that he had sacrificed his daughter's life for nothing – a conviction which still further exacerbated his basic dislike of Napoleon. He was also – unreasonably – inclined to blame Cavour for these misfortunes, but in this case the Prime Minister showed an unusual understanding. 'In other circumstances,' he wrote to a friend, 'I should not have borne patiently such bitter reproofs (but) I have put him at the foot of the horrible calvary on which diplomacy prepares once more to crucify Italy.'

Napoleon's apologia was received the day following the demand for disarmament. In it he said that he had been forced to agree to the exclusion of Piedmont from the conference table because of pressure from the other powers, and also 'to gain time', but, alarmingly, he seemed to be adding his voice to those demanding demobilization and the basic reduction of Piedmont's already too small army. 'England and Prussia insist,' he wrote lamely, while adding that similar demands had been put to Austria.

Cavour reacted quickly. With the approval of Victor Emmanuel, he left for Paris four days later, having received a telegram from 'Plon-Plon' (who after his marriage had shown himself to be an ardent supporter of his wife's country in all matters) not only that would he be welcome but that the Emperor himself had, with difficulty, gained for him a seat at the congress.

The Prime Minister spent four busy days in the French

capital having long talks with representatives of all the major powers with the exception of Austria. These talks were conducted on a generally friendly basis even though from the start Cavour made it plain that disarmament was out of the question. The most heated arguments occurred when he was alone with Walewski, when the French Foreign Minister insisted that Napoleon was determined to stay at peace with Austria and to extricate himself from 'the tangle of Italian affairs', to which Cavour replied that he must have 'misunderstood' his master's promises. The next day there was a final interview with Napoleon in which the Emperor again stressed that it was a question of exercising patience but that all would eventually go according to plan. Cavour, however, was not altogether happy as rather than his having the expected *tête-à-tête* with the Emperor, Walewski, though silent, was present.

On arriving back in Turin, Cavour's first act was to write to Napoleon stressing two points. Firstly he reiterated that disarmament was quite out of the question, since this would spell the collapse of the official resistance and probably that of the Government, as well letting in the malcontents and revolutionaries to inaugurate a period of political chaos, if not anarchy. On the other hand, if it could be confirmed that Piedmont was to be allowed to take her place at the congress, *with or without* representatives from the other Italian states, a limited disarmament might be possible. As a concrete proposal he put forward the suggestion that, if Austria reduced her army to its pre-1 January (1859) strength and dismantled the Piacenza fortifications, Piedmont would be prepared to disband the reserves and non-Piedmontese-volunteers. As his second point, he argued that Piedmont had a *legal* right to a seat at the congress based on a clause contained in the Treaty of Aix-la-Chapelle of 1818. The letter was accompanied by a passionate personal appeal to the Emperor not to abandon his ally Victor Emmanuel.

It is believed that Napoleon was deeply moved. Yet his position had become if anything more complicated, more thwart with danger, than that even of the King. He was having to contend not only with the latent hostility of his neighbours and the very real threat that Prussian armies might cross the Rhine if French troops crossed the Alps, but also with the growing strength of the anti-war party in France itself, both in governmental circles, and in the powerful *bourgeoisie*.

In the meantime, though still determined not to be open to the accusation of having fired the first shot, the Austrians continued to act as though war were inevitable. The 6th and 9th Army Corps were brought up to war establishment, and all senior officers in Italy were warned that hostilities might break out by the 20th of the month (April). When the energetic Lord Malmesbury proposed that the two countries in contention should withdraw their forces some ten miles from the Piedmont-Lombardy frontier, Victor Emmanuel agreed, but Count Buol was able to persuade Franz Josef to refuse, the excuse being that Austria had given her official word that she had no aggressive intentions regarding Piedmont.

Despite this refusal, very unfairly, it was Piedmont who remained the object of both British and Prussian ire. Lord Cowley is reliably reported as having confided in Baron Hubner: 'You ought to summon Piedmont to disarm, cross the frontier, destroy her, and then declare you are ready to negotiate in Congress when and where we like.' To which Hubner replied: 'That is what we ought to do, and probably will.'

Count Gyulai – who must have been praying that he would not find himself at the head of an army fighting a real, shooting war – composed a sabre-rattling manifesto which he ordered to be read in all barracks and transmitted to the Turin newspapers, evidently hoping that it would have an intimidating effect.

Soldiers! His Majesty the Emperor summons you to the standards in order to abase for the third time the conceit of Piedmont and to hunt from their lair the fanatical subverters of the general tranquillity of Europe.

Soldiers of every rank! You are going against an army which you have always put to flight. It is useless to recommend discipline and courage to you for your discipline is unique in the world and in courage no army surpasses you.

In spite of such bellicose proclamations, Lord Malmesbury (anticipating the role which Chamberlain would play in 1938 at Munich by bullying comparatively weak Czechoslovakia into submitting to the outrageous demands of Hitler in order to obtain 'peace in our time') was determined to have the last word, above all on the principle of Piedmont's disarmament. His success now hinged on pressurizing France to browbeat her ally – her ally in name only, as it must have seemed at the time. To this end there was a dramatic meeting in the Tuileries on the evening of 18 April, when Napoleon was mercilessly badgered by his own Foreign Minister, Walewski, grimly backed by Lord Cowley and Baron Hubner. Though Count Nigra and 'Plon-Plon' were also present to speak for Piedmont, the overpowering force represented by the opposition was too much for Napoleon.

That same night a despatch was sent to Turin with the news that France also was insisting on Piedmont's disarmament before her voice could be heard at the coming congress.

The French Ambassador in Turin, to whom the message was addressed, was ordered to proceed immediately to Cavour's residence to inform him of the decision. The Ambassador, however, was in no mood to turn out so late at night. Instead he sent his private secretary.

According to Count Orsi, 'The Minister (Cavour) had retired to bed, but on being told of this unusual visit directed that the secretary be shown into his room. There, sitting on the bed, he read the unlucky telegram. It seemed to him that he had been abandoned by France, and he feared that he had drawn his country into ruin. His grief was so great that he exclaimed – "There is nothing left for me but to blow my brains out with a pistol".'

Next morning the French Ambassador called on the broken Prime Minister to be handed a brief written statement: 'Since France joins England in demanding the preventive disarmament of Piedmont, the King's Government, although it foresees that this provision will have the most calamitous effects for the tranquillity of Italy, declares its readiness to comply.'

One can imagine the brutal impact that this apparent betrayal must have had on a man of Cavour's temperament. He gave evidence of being on the verge of a total breakdown. Having, with the King's permission, compiled the statement which the Ambassador immediately transmitted to Paris, he shut himself up in his study, giving strict orders that nobody should be allowed in to see him. Any moment it was feared, he might indeed 'blow his brains out with a pistol'. Finally a great personal friend, a certain Michelangelo Castelli, decided to ignore the request that he be left alone. Brushing aside the protesting servants, Castelli found the Prime Minister slumped at his desk tearing up papers. A fire, obviously fed by the shredded documents, burned fiercely.

It was Castelli who broke the silence.

'I know that nobody was supposed to enter this room,' he said, 'but I have come for that very reason. Am I to believe that Count Cavour is going to desert the field before the battle?'

The two men stared at each other. Suddenly Cavour got to his feet, embraced his friend and smiled. The crisis was over.

'Let us be calm,' he said. 'We will face everything and always be together.'

It seems incredible that any government, having scored a complete, and basically undeserved, diplomatic victory, the result of which was to reduce a potential enemy to impotency without the necessity of firing a shot, should then proceed to throw away the fruits of this victory by what can only be described as an act of crass stupidity, reversing world opinion overnight, to become the sinner rather than the sinned against! Yet this is just what the Austrian ruler did, and as Franz Josef was always at pains to make it abundantly clear that he was an absolute monarch embodying the principle of 'L'état c'est moi', he must accept the full burden of guilt, even though he would endeavour to lay the blame on his two evil advisers, Count Grunne and Count Buol.

On 12 April Buol informed Lord Malmesbury that Austria intended to demand *immediate* Piedmontese disarmament, to receive the reply that Britain would approve of such a demand only if Austria were prepared to follow suit. This British reply reached Vienna the same day, 12 April. It was ignored, since Buol had been able to persuade the Emperor that, no matter what the circumstances, if Austria were to be engaged in a shooting war with Piedmont, her army would take the field reinforced by contingents from both Britain and Prussia. Thus, in spite of Victor Emmanuel's despairing acquiescence to the demand put to him by the man on whom he had counted as a whole-hearted ally, the Austrian Government set about composing a veritable ultimatum which arrived in Turin the night of 23 April.

It was 5.30 p.m. when Baron Kellersberg handed Cavour the document, which ended:

> I have the honour to beg Your Excellency to inform me whether the King consents, yes or no, to put the army on a peace footing without delay and to disband the Italian volunteers. The bearer of this letter, to whom Your Excellency will please deliver your answer, has instructions to hold himself at your disposal for that purpose during three days. If at the end of that time he has received no reply, or if the reply is not completely satisfactory, the responsibility of the grave consequences that may follow from this refusal will fall entirely on the government of His Sardinian Majesty. After trying in vain every conciliatory means of procuring for his people the guarantee of peace on which the Emperor is entitled to insist, His Majesty will be obliged, with great regret, to resort to force of arms in order to obtain it.

Neither Victor Emmanuel nor Cavour could believe their good fortune. Just at the moment when after so many years of 'sweat and tears' all had seemed lost, an act of near unbelievable folly on the part of the Austrian Emperor had played straight into their hands. There could be no possible argument. The document presented by Baron Kellersberg amounted to a declaration of war. No other interpretation was possible.

Cavour was instructed to make an appointment with the Baron exactly three days later in order to offer an official rejection of the demands, and at the same time to telegraph the text to Paris accompanied by a formal request that Napoleon fulfil the promises given at Plombières, now entirely justified by the naked threat from Vienna.

Thus, by this one act of unconsidered folly, Austria had

thrown away all the advantages gained over the last few months. She now stood before the world as a wanton aggressor. Britain was outraged. Prussia realized that any attempt to interfere with the French in their determination to spring to the aid of 'gallant little Piedmont' would draw on her head the wrath not only of Britain but of Russia.

Twenty-four hours' intense propaganda were enough to rout the anti-war party in France itself. Soon the whole country was clamouring for action. Napoleon's statement that 'by declaring war on Piedmont, Austria had declared war on France' met with universal approval. The departure for the front had about it something of the occasion of a public festival of rejoicing. On 10 May, riding at the head of the Imperial Guard from the Tuileries to the Gare de Lyon where he boarded a train for Toulon, from there to embark for Genoa, Napoleon was greeted by frenzied shouts of *'Vive la Guerre!'* from huge crowds, mostly of workmen, massed on the pavements. The carriage bearing the Empress Eugénie, appointed Regent during the Emperor's absence, and the little Prince Imperial, dressed in a miniature Guard's uniform, could only progress at a snail's pace and was pelted with flowers.

Franz Josef was completely taken by surprise and indeed appalled by the storm his ultimatum aroused. Seeking a scapegoat – unjustly – he dismissed Count Buol for what was, after all, his own abysmal lack of political comprehension. He must have suspected that he had committed a most colossal error of judgement, for the day after the ultimatum had been despatched, and before reactions to it became known, he called on the aged Metternich, who was living in retirement in the Rennweg. The former all-powerful Chancellor was then eighty-six years old and extremely feeble physically, though his brain had remained remarkably clear. His first remark on hearing of the document was, 'For Heaven's sake, send no ultimatum to Italy!' To which the rather chastened young Emperor was obliged to reply, 'It was despatched yesterday.'

Buol's dismissal did nothing to attenuate the immense harm done, any more than did a diplomatic visit of apology to Berlin undertaken by the Archduke Albert. Nothing could now avert the outbreak of war – the war of the Emperor's own making.

In a vague way Franz Josef tried to justify himself in an even longer proclamation than that which, on his orders, had been issued by Gyulai and which began: 'I have ordered my faithful and valiant army to put an end to the attacks lately carried to the extreme degree which the neighbouring State of Sardinia is directing against the incontestable rights of my Crown and the inviolability of the Empire entrusted to me by God. I have thus fulfilled my painful but unavoidable duty as the head of the State.' He then went on to complain that his extreme generosity to that same state of Sardinia, soundly defeated in two wars with Austria's armed forces, had resulted not in any show of gratitude on the part of the vanquished but, on the contrary, in an unrelenting hostility and continued encouragement of subversive anti-Austrian activity. An attack on France followed, with a warning that the spirit of revolution would be banished by 'Providence', whose weapon, as in the past before similar threats, would be 'the sword of Austria'. He ended by appealing for the loyalty and support of all his people: 'Give me in the struggle that we are engaged in, your long-proved fidelity, your self-abnegation, your devotion. To your sons whom I have called into the ranks of the army, I, their captain, send a martial salute. Entrusted to them the Austrian Eagle will carry high its glorious flight.'

In Piedmont enthusiasm was at its height. For the Piedmontese, monarchist and republican, conservative and liberal, nobleman and peasant, for all alike, it was 'their finest hour'. Cavour's speech in the Chamber of Deputies, after outlining the history of the crisis, called for full powers to be conferred on the King for the defence of the country for so long as the war might last. 'Who,' he demanded, 'can be a better guardian of our liberties? Who more worthy of the Nation's trust? He whose name throughout ten years of reign has been synonymous with loyalty and honour. He who now holds high, as always, the tricolor of Italy.'

Victor Emmanuel, for his part, was anxious to enter the field. More than ever he was taking a pride in his popular title of 'the Soldier King', and prayed that he might justify it. He was not altogether happy at the idea of handing over supreme command to the French Emperor, but he had the good sense to realize that, in view of the immense effort that the French would be putting into the campaign and the size of the force they would be committing, it was very much a question of the adage 'He who pays the piper calls the tune.'

On receiving the full powers Cavour had demanded for him, his first act was to issue a call to the army. *'Io sarò vostra duce sul campo dell' onore e della gloria. Voi, ne sono certo, saprete conservare, anzi accrescere, la vostra fama di prodi soldati.'* ('I will be your leader on the field of honour and of glory. You, I know, will preserve, even add to, your renown as gallant soldiers.') He ended: 'March on then, confident of victory and with fresh laurels decorate your standard. With its three colours, and with the flower of Italy's youth drawn up beneath it, that standard proclaims to you that your task is the achievement of Italian independence. It is a just and sacred task, and it shall be our battle cry!'

Though the ultimate goal was not achieved as rapidly as he had hoped, and expected, Cavour's words to the Chamber of Deputies before conveying the Government's reply to Baron Kellersberg were prophetic: 'I leave the last sitting of the Piedmontese Parliament,' he said. 'The next will be that of the kingdom of Italy!'

Part Two
INTO BATTLE

7

Advance to Magenta

More than an era passed with Napoleon's defeat at Waterloo. In Europe generalship became a vanished art. The subtle skills of manoeuvre and planning were reduced to a minimum, as the Crimea had demonstrated. Yet despite the inertia which seemed to threaten the battlefield, rare occasions did present themselves for a commander worthy of the name, such as Radetsky, to gain a spectacular success by vigorous application of the principle of initiative, especially in the opening phases of a campaign, and such an occasion was offered to Count Gyulai in the closing days of April.

The Austrian army in Lombardy, of which Gyulai had taken reluctant command, numbered just over a hundred thousand men. It was not up to full strength, and its effectives were to be doubled almost within a few weeks. Nevertheless, on the day formal hostilities broke out, the Austrians outnumbered the Piedmontese by at least two to one. Ordered by Franz Josef to eliminate Piedmontese resistance before a link-up with the French took place, Gyulai had concentrated his forces along the east bank of the Ticino river, running north-south till its confluence with the Po just below Pavia, only some sixty miles as the crow flies from Turin. Though intensively cultivated, the country between Turin and the Ticino is monotonously flat. A determined drive west could have brought the Austrian army to the city gates within a few days, certainly before the first French soldier could have reached the scene of action.

Gyulai's hesitations are incomprehensible. His orders were amply clear. He cannot be accused of executing them ineptly. He did nothing! Technically speaking, he could have been court-martialled for disobedience, and he could count himself lucky that, other than to relieve him of his command, no action was taken against him for his mulish timidity since its results were disastrous. A campaign which might have been won decisively within a few days was as decisively lost within a few weeks.

There is a tendency to minimize Gyulai's defects by underlining that he was a misfit and by recalling the fact that he had begged to be passed over for command. This is true but constitutes no excuse for his failure to act on orders once he found himself *in situ*, his country's destiny in his hands, or for his tactical handling of the situation – when at last he did make a move – which would have disgraced a newly commissioned second lieutenant. It is also said that diplomatic confusion as to the likely attitudes of Prussia and Britain weighed on his mind, but a soldier who bases his field tactics on possible political developments is guilty not only of near treason but of moral cowardice. Still more misleading in the assessment of Gyulai's conduct is the suggestion that the decision to take the offensive immediately would have 'called for not merely competence but for the aggressive self-confidence found only as a rule in fools or great captains'. On the contrary one had to be either a fool or cursed with excessive pusillanimity not to do so under the circumstances. Admiral Byng was shot for a far less heinous crime, but rigid as was Franz Josef's outlook, he was never prepared to go to such lengths *pour encourager les autres*.

Gyulai had five army corps and a cavalry division at his disposal: Victor Emmanuel had five divisions and a cavalry brigade. Furthermore the Austrian commander knew that massive reinforcements were on their way, and it would be mid-May, his advisers reckoned, before French troops could enter the line beside their Piedmontese allies. Again, it should be pointed out that the Austrian troops embarked on the campaign with a strong feeling of superiority, remembering the victories of 1848 and 1849. Many men who had participated in these successes still served in the ranks. On the other hand the army's polyethnic composition did constitute a weakness: 'Croat regiments ... Czech dragoons and German Uhlans, and Magyar light horsemen ... Hungarian grenadiers and Serbs from the eastern frontiers ...' Nor could the possibility be overlooked that some of the non-German speakers, especially the Hungarians with their own yearning for independence, might well be in sympathy with those they were called upon to fight. Even so, a rapid success, the speedy occupation of Turin, could so easily have turned 1859 into a second 1849.

When eventually, after pointless marching and counter-marching up and down the east bank, Gyulai began a slow crossing of the Ticino on 8 May, he had still not made up his mind as to his objective. Should he strike at Turin, or turn on the main Piedmontese forces concentrated in the neighbourhood of Alessandria south of the Po?

Turin, without a doubt, should have been the target. The fall of a capital city usually deals the adversary's morale a shattering blow – if one can forget 1812 and Moscow. The city in his hands would have split his enemy in two before the junction of their two wings could have been effected. And although combined Franco-Piedmontese forces enjoyed numerical superiority, pivoting on a central position, he could have fallen on and destroyed each wing separately, exploiting his own local superiority in numbers and taking advantage of the lack of co-ordination so often characterizing an allied command in its early stages.

As soon as the Austrian main body was over the river, and as if to punish Gyulai for his dilatoriness, rain began to fall in torrents. Roads and tracks turned into quagmires overnight. Radetsky would have been frantic, urging his men through the mud. Gyulai, on the contrary, welcomed the freak weather since it prevented him from moving quickly and provided a providential excuse with which to reply to telegrams reproaching him for his inactivity. Nevertheless, though unbelievable slow, progress was steady and the forward elements of the vanguard were already in Novara on the approaches to Allessandria when suddenly the order to halt was given. There was a brief pause, then, to the amazement and fury of most of the junior commanders, the army was turned about and hurried back to the Ticino's east bank to take up roughly the same positions from which it had set out – like 'all the King's horses and the King's men', they had been marched across the river and then back again. Later Gyulai's explanation for this final blunder was that, 'Failing to bump into the opposition he expected, receiving alarming tidings of a large French force already on the way from Turin to Alessandria, knowing that his northern flank was threatened by the Piedmontese between him and the northern spurs of the Appenines, he decided that Turin, which lay virtually open, must in fact be heavily defended.'

By 2 June the whole of the Austrian army was back in Lombardy.

Canrobert's 3rd Corps was the first French formation to set foot in Italy. '*Il nous faut arriver avec la rapidité de la foudre*' ('We must get there at the speed of lightning'), Napoleon had insisted, and the Marshal had done his best to obey the injunction. Setting out from Lyon, his corps marched over the 6,500-foot Mont Cenis Pass in weather imposing a severe strain on the men's physical resistance. Moreover, for the sake of speed they marched light. Essential camping material was left behind, entailing great hardship during the bitter nights at high altitudes. There were no proper reserves of either food or ammunition; the artillery was cut to an absolute minimum. The propaganda effect, however, was of primary importance. For the Piedmontese the sight of the long columns of French troops winding down the southern slopes was visible proof of Napoleon's determination to fulfil his obligations to the hilt.

A messenger, announcing that the vanguard was already in the neighbourhood of Susa, reached a delighted Victor Emmanuel just as he was on the point of setting out for Alessandria. 'Please tell the Emperor', he said to the messenger, a certain Captain Brady of Irish descent, 'to excuse me for not sending a reply in writing. At this moment I am off to put myself at the head of my army. And when you see Marshal Canrobert, beg him to send me a regiment. I intend to throw up field fortifications in front of Casale and it is of vital importance that Gyulai sees the red trousers interspersed with the working parties.'*

---

* A reference to the baggy red trousers worn by French infantry of the line regiments.

Victor Emmanuel had every reason to be delighted. Those early May days were amongst the most anxious of his whole life. Already he knew that, had he rather than Gyulai been in command those first weeks, he might well have finished the war, victoriously, almost before it had begun. He could not stop thanking God that Radetsky had died and praying that Napoleon did indeed fully appreciate the need for speed, and yet more speed.

Not wishing to expose his army to the risk of annihilation at one blow, he split his force, concentrating the bulk round Alessandria, a bare eighty miles from Genoa, so as to facilitate liaison with the French contingent which would be arriving by sea from Toulon, leaving the road to Turin virtually unguarded. Far better, in his opinion, to lose a city, even the capital, than see his fighting potential destroyed. It was largely for this reason that he had decided to take personal command. The coming war, as he saw it, would decide not only Piedmont's future, her very existence, but that of a future Italy. Victory could, almost certainly would, herald the birth of the 'kingdom of Italy'; defeat would spell the destruction of the embryo of independence. At such a moment it would be unjust, he felt, for any other than himself to be in a position to take the fateful decisions in moments of crisis which must inevitably arise in the course of the next few weeks.

The bulk of the French army transported by sea to Genoa began arriving at the rate of some five thousand a day from 3 May onwards. On disembarkation, the troops moved directly to a vast tented area situated to the north and west of the city. Napoleon landed on the 12th, spent a couple of days on a tour of inspection, then moved to Alessandria to assume, as had been pre-arranged, supreme command of the allied armies.

By 18 May there were 107,656 French soldiers in Italy, six slightly under-strength army corps, commanded by Marshals Canrobert and Baraguey d'Hilliers, and Generals MacMahon, Niel and Regnault de St-Jean d'Angely. According to General Zédé, then a junior officer in the Foreign Legion and author of a detailed diary of the campaign, the 6th Corps, entrusted to Prince Napoleon, the Emperor's cousin 'Plon-Plon', was always referred to as 'the fifth wheel' because 'it never did anything'.

There was a novel feature about the new Napoleonic army: the size of the contingent from North Africa. These veterans of the Sahara and the oases had fought in comparatively small numbers outside Sebastopol, but among the troops who marched north from Genoa was an entire corps, the 2nd, commanded by MacMahon, made up of tough 'Africans' – Foreign Legion, *Chasseurs d'Afrique*, Zouaves, *Tirailleurs Algériens* – eager to prove that it was they who formed the hard core of the expeditionary force, and to outshine in battle the Imperial Guard whose brilliant uniforms, unchanged since Wagram – and especially the Grenadiers in their tall bearskins, had made such a deep impression on the local inhabitants.

General Zédé records that there was a considerable amount of badinage, not always good-humoured, exchanged between the 'Africans' and the Guards. On the march up to Alessandria, a resplendently uniformed trooper of the Guards called out to a legionary, 'Hi, there, little foot soldier, wouldn't you like to be in my place?' 'Not a bit,' the legionary shouted back. 'I'd rather be your horse. Then you'd have to wash my arse every morning!' Not at all amused the Guard drew his sabre, whereupon the legionary, a rugged little Parisian who had enlisted under the false name of Tetu and of Swiss nationality, jabbed the horse in the rump with his bayonet. The charger gave a great bound and bucked madly, throwing its rider to the accompaniment of Legion jeers.

Napoleon himself was now fifty-one years of age. Unlike Victor Emmanuel, he had no experience of warfare on the grand scale. The combats in which he had fought bravely as a youth with the Carbonari could not compare in magnitude with Novara or Custozza. Yet he had always been profoundly interested in the science of warfare and had studied his uncle's campaigns – especially the Italian campaigns – down to the last available detail. Now, remembering how boldness had brought about such signal and speedy triumphs, he was determined to take a leaf out of the book of his great predecessor.

Having reached agreement with Victor Emmanuel that the first major objective should be Milan, he proposed switching the entire main body from the southern to the northern sector so as to strike direct at the Lombard capital along the axis of the road running from Novara via the small town of Magenta on the east bank of the Ticino.

To accomplish this he would be obliged, as a preliminary, to execute one of the most dangerous manoeuvres in the military textbook: a flank march parallel with the enemy's front.

In the meantime Gyulai committed yet another blunder. Thinking that the allies' first objective would be the stronghold of Piacenza, he ordered a general advance along the south bank of the Po. But again he could not bring himself to engage the bulk of his army, and the advance boiled down to a reconnaissance in force by Count Stadion's corps aimed at Voghera.

On 20 May Stadion's twenty-thousand-strong corps ran into an infinitely smaller allied formation, General Forey's division of Baraguey d'Hillier's 1st Corps, supported by a regiment of the Novara light horse, at Montebello, due south of Pavia and some twenty miles east of Alessandria.

Despite their being outnumbered by at least three to one, this first encounter of the war ended in the favour of the allies. Throughout the day General Forey's handling of his force displayed a high standard of generalship. It was as though for an instant the mantle of the great Napoleon had fallen on his shoulders. Though he realized immediately that a full enemy corps opposed him, he made up his mind to attack, ordering his right wing of five weak battalions to the Genestrello heights and Genestrello village occupied by an Austrian division. Storming forward on the left, two other French battalions crashed head on into two Austrian regiments holding Gambovo and were saved from annihilation only by the intervention of four squadrons of the light horse who did not hesitate to charge the entrenched Austrian infantry. Their repeated attacks finally broke through the defences, forcing the Austrians to fall back in near total disorder to Casteggio, while the French infantry, who had carried Genestrello at the point of the bayonet, closed in on Montebello, which was in turn stormed after a succession of bayonet charges.

Dismayed by the fighting spirit of both French and Piedmontese, and by their willingness to carry the fight to an opponent so greatly outnumbering them, the Austrian retreat, slow to begin with, came near to deteriorating into a *sauve qui peut*. The Franco-Piedmontese lost two excellent leaders, Lieutenant-Colonel Morelli, killed while leading a charge of his Monferrate squadron, and a regimental commander, Colonel Beuret, but their total casualties were less than one third of those of the Austrians.

This minor success acted as a great stimulant to allied morale. It was the first time, almost within living memory, that the Piedmontese had participated in a clear-cut victory over the traditional enemy, while for the French it was an omen, for in 1800 Lannes had won a hard-fought battle at Montebello over the Austrians prior to the great victory of Marengo. It also helped to improve relations between French troops and the local populations, for though Napoleon himself had received a tremendous welcome from the Genoese, his troops had been complaining bitterly about the behaviour of villagers who, they said, were treating them as though they were foreign invaders rather than allies risking death for their freedom.

The truth, which the French found hard to grasp, was that a significant proportion of Piedmontese were heartily sick of war and in addition feared that defeat might spell the end of their privileged status as the only region in Italy to be ruled by an Italian. More than in the cause of eventual Italian unity, they were interested in the maintenance of their own independence. Its loss was something they could not contemplate with equanimity. But when the news, greatly embellished, of victory at Montebello was propagated, doubts gave way to soaring optimism, still further fanned when, a few days later, there came reports of a second, and considerably more important, success at Palestro.

After Montebello, the main body of the French army moved north to Vercelli; just south of Novara, where it was the intention to cross the Sesia river, then swing east, aiming directly at Milan. The move was something of a gamble, but a gamble which came off. Gyulai failed to fall on the dangerously exposed French flank. Instead he withdrew most of the covering force he had left on the Ticino's west bank, leaving only a small rearguard to protect this further retrograde movement concentrated round the village of Palestro.

Throughout the march north, both Napoleon and Victor Emmanuel were fully aware of the risks they ran, and it was to shield the final stage that the Piedmontese, bolstered by a Zouave regiment, were ordered to cross the Sesia and seize Palestro on 30 May. This in itself was a highly hazardous operation. The Sesia was swollen by melting snows and recent heavy rain, and its banks were steep. In the Palestro area there were only two practical means of crossing the angry stream: by a ford reported to be dangerously deep, and by a bridge only just wide enough for two men to march abreast. The Austrians had not thought it worth while to blow the bridge, but both it and the ford were covered by their artillery.

The honours of the battle's first stage were carried off by the Zouaves who led the attack. Bayonets fixed, two companies waded the ford, while another two swarmed across the bridge in the face of a hail of cannon and small arms fire, clearing a bridgehead by the use of cold steel alone with such élan that the admiring Piedmontese coined the phrase, so much quoted from then on, 'la furia francese'. Following close on the Zouaves' heels, General Cialdini was able to occupy Palestro village with his division, but he barely had time to consolidate before being violently counter-attacked. Austrian efforts to recapture so vital a position were kept up till well after nightfall, then renewed at first light on the 31st, not being broken off till one division, that of Count Szabo had been virtually wiped out, but the Piedmontese and Zouaves stood firm.

Ferocious as the combat had been, one little incident showed that a certain spirit of chivalry survived even as late as the mid-nineteenth century.

After the battle an Austrian artillery officer recalled how he had been knocked senseless by a Zouave's rifle butt. When he recovered his senses, he found himself being propped up by the same Zouave, who was holding a wine-filled water-bottle to his lips, saying soothingly, 'Buvez un coup, mon capitaine. Ca vous remettra!' ('Have a drop, captain. It'll put you on your feet again!')

On both days Victor Emmanuel showed himself worthy to be called 'the soldier king'. Wherever the fighting was thickest, he was to be found encouraging his men, showing a remarkable disdain for danger as bullets whizzed past him. The Zouaves were deeply impressed. Reviving an old custom, as a result of which the first Napoleon had won the affectionate nickname of '*le petit caporal*', they offered the King, much to his delight, the two plain woollen stripes, conferring on him the title of 'honorary corporal of the 3rd Zouaves'.

Thanks to this hard-fought action, the main body of the French army covered the last stage of its approach march unopposed, then, regrouping to face east, advanced rapidly on the Ticino.

The stage was now set for the first of the campaign's two major battles, that which took its name from the small town of Magenta, a couple of miles to the east of the river, astride the main road and commanding the railway. It was purely a French battle, a fact which gave rise to considerable ill feeling as well as controversy, putting a severe strain on the all too flimsy ties binding the two allies.

According to most French commentators, the French, from the Emperor down to the most junior private soldier, believed that the Piedmontese had deliberately held back, that they were in fact prepared to fight 'to the last Frenchman'. This bitterness was aggravated when the casualties became known. A.J. Whyte, however, in *The political life and letters of Cavour*, after pointing out that Napoleon was never on good terms with the King, added: 'There is evidence that he (Napoleon) was not without jealousy of Victor Emmanuel ... After Palestro, which was mainly a Piedmontese victory, Napoleon took care to keep his allies posted in reserve at Galliate during the battle of Magenta, to the intense annoyance of Victor Emmanuel ever impatient for action.'

There is no denying that Victor Emmanuel was a fire-eater. That he should have deliberately avoided the action is inconceivable, yet it is more than unlikely that Napoleon, always fearful of the effect at home of a long casualty list, should, equally deliberately, have kept the Piedmontese from the battlefield. One approaches the truth, in all probability, by recognizing that neither King nor Emperor, brave as they were under fire, had the basic military talent or necessary experience to handle vast armies so that the complicated wheels of the staff machine should run smoothly. Like their opponent, the Emperor Franz Josef, they would have made excellent regimental commanders, but they were totally out of their depth when called upon to co-ordinate the movements of masses of up to 200,000 men. As regards Napoleon, a contemporary confirmed – though one feels he may have been exaggerating – that 'the Emperor could not read a map intelligently, master the movement of troops in the field, or grasp the course of events'.

The battle of Magenta was won more by good luck than good judgement, and this being the case, it is more than likely that Victor Emmanuel's move to the battlefield was impeded by confused orders and their equally confused execution. Furthermore, to give some credence to this theory, one can read in Italian military histories that 'the nearest Piedmontese division to the scene of action was delayed by the indecision of its commander, General Fanti'.

Coherent command was further complicated by the fact that the terrain caused almost insuperable difficulties in keeping a tight control on movement. It has been described as 'for the fighting man the closest in the world; for the farmer the richest'. And the commentator adds: 'Flat as your hand it stretches to infinity, every inch under intensive cultivation and marvellously irrigated. Long unbroken lines of mulberry trees and heavily looped elms serve as the supports for carefully trained vines, and in between these narrow lanes the rich earth is cultivated in long strips ... the country is virtually impassable except by lanes serving the farms; two squadrons of cavalry could pass in broad daylight within fifteen yards of each other without being any the wiser.' Under the circumstances the closeness of the country was an advantage for the French in that it minimized the Austrians' cavalry superiority and gave scope for the initiative and greater tactical skill of French junior officers and NCOs.

Finding the bridges intact, MacMahon, on the left flank, was able to cross the Ticino at two points in the neighbourhood of Turbigo on 3 June. The principal axis of the French advance, however, was the main road further south, and this Gyulai endeavoured to deny to his enemy by the establishment of a strong defensive position on the west bank beyond Trecate, known as the San Martino bridgehead.

The principle was sound, but the local commander, misreading his orders, thought that he was supposed to dig in on the east bank. Abandoning the San Martino redoubt, leaving behind considerable stores of ammunition and a number of pieces of artillery, he withdrew his force to the east bank. He then proceeded to make matters worse by installing his new position too far behind the actual river and the canal running parallel with it effectively to oppose the French crossing.

MacMahon knew nothing of this but nevertheless exploited his unexpectedly easy passage of the Ticino by occupying Turbigo itself. Three battalions of *Tirailleurs Algériens* then pushed forward in the direction of Robecchetto, where they bumped into an Austrian column groping its way through the thick country. Emulating the Zouaves at Palestro, the Algerians threw the Austrians back to Robecchetto itself, then cleared the village after a series of bayonet charges and pushed on a further mile. They had not fired a single shot, they claimed proudly. It had been cold steel, and cold steel only, all the way.

As night was by then falling, MacMahon called a halt.

The same evening Napoleon issued his orders for the following day. MacMahon's 2nd Corps was to continue a limited advance at dawn, then swing south in the direction of Magenta. The Imperial Guard, the 1st, 3rd and 4th Corps were also to drive on Magenta, crossing the Ticino and the Sforzesca Canal by the main bridge, Ponte-nuovo-di-Buffalora, below Buffalora village. The French Emperor had no idea as to his enemy's exact whereabouts, an ignorance he shared with Gyulai, who, though expecting the French advance to the east bank and not knowing that his orders had been so hopelessly misinterpreted, was confident that the San Martino redoubt would hold. With the arrival of reinforcements awaited hourly, he believed that he would be able to execute a pincer movement to catch the French main body between the two arms with the wide Ticino at their backs.

It would be difficult to find a more classic example of the

much-used phrase 'the fog of war'.

By the morning of 4 June, Gyulai's command had increased to a formidable strength of close on 160,000, but for a number of reasons he was never able to concentrate this mass at any given moment. If his original advance had been slow, in contrast his retreat had been unduly hurried, carried out mostly by forced marches. Units were scattered and had lost communication with those on their flanks. In addition the men were exhausted, in many cases weak with hunger due to the near total breakdown of the notoriously inefficient commissariat. When battle was joined, Austrian units straggled haphazardly into combat, acting mostly on their own initiative, and although the struggle lasted some thirty-six hours before Gyulai panicked, admitted defeat and ordered an even more precipitate retreat to the east of the Mincio, a bare two-thirds of his total effectives had been engaged.

At dawn (the 4th), the 2nd and 3rd Grenadiers of the Guard were astonished to find the massive San Martino redoubt abandoned. Reinforced by the 1st Grenadiers, the Zouaves of the Guard and a regiment of horse artillery, they then pushed on to cross the river unopposed. Once on the east bank, however, the Guards were pinned down by heavy fire from the Austrian artillery till midday, at which time the sound of battle from the direction of Turbigo encouraged Napoleon to believe that MacMahon's flanking movement must be making good progress, and to order a frontal attack on San Martino village by General Mellinet's Guards division.

The major obstacle to the advance was an improvised bunker constructed round the railway bridge where the line south to Buffalora was crossed by the Trecate-Magenta road at Naviglio. Strong though the position was, it fell to a mass bayonet charge thrown in by all three Grenadier regiments, but once the last of the defenders had either been bayoneted or surrendered, the Grenadiers were again halted by Austrian batteries concentrated on the outskirts of Magenta. Pinned down, Mellinet's battalions were then subjected to a series of determined counter-attacks, but though heavily outnumbered, the Guards held Naviglio long enough to allow Niel and Canrobert to deploy their corps and MacMahon to complete his turning movement from the north. A notable casualty at this stage was General Cler of the Zouaves of the Guard, killed leading a charge.

The 85th of the line, commanded by Colonel de Bellecourt, of General Vinoy's division (3rd Corps), was the first to reinforce the hard-pressed Guards.

I found General de Wimpffen* of the Imperial Guard (says de Bellecourt in his memoirs) who had a cheek skinned by a bullet. He told me to send one of my battalions to the canal bridge. I clambered up the embankment to my right, only just in time; the Austrians were a bare twenty paces from the railway bridge. I drew my sword and shouted 'A moi le 85 ième'. In a matter of seconds my men had climbed the embankment like cats and we charged with the bayonet. We threw the Austrians back into the village of Ponte-di-Magenta; after savage street fighting we took 3 or 400 prisoners. But I hadn't many men left for my regiment had been cruelly depleted and it was essential not to give up an inch of ground we had won. Austrian reinforcements came charging up each side of the canal, and Austrian sharpshooters on the roofs took a heavy toll of our officers. To make matters worse they began to shell us and we hadn't a single gun with which to reply.

Even so the regiment clung on to its positions till, later in the afternoon, 'Marshal Canrobert suddenly appeared in our midst. One of his horses had been wounded, and his chief of staff, Colonel de Senneville, killed. The Marshal was riding a white horse and bullets hummed round him.' By seven o'clock in the evening most of MacMahon's corps had arrived on the scene, and the Austrians, maintaining good order, pulled back into the town of Magenta itself, an agglomeration of some four thousand inhabitants, converting it into a fortress.

The attack on Magenta was entrusted to the 2nd Corps after the Guards had been moved back into reserve, much to their disgust, for rivalry between the 'Parisians' and the 'Africans' had been further exacerbated by the fighting and the badinage mentioned by Zédé showed no signs of abating even under such grim conditions.

From the moment that darkness began to spread over the

---

* Not to be confused with General von Wimpffen of the Austrian army.

countryside, and until the early hours of the 5th, Magenta developed into yet another 'soldiers' battle' after the pattern of Inkerman. All that counted during those hours was individual strength, individual courage, the will to vanquish, the willingness to die rather than yield. Had history's greatest captains been present, it is doubtful if they could have affected the issue. In this brutal struggle to the death, all that a commander could do was to join in the fray himself, and many did.

MacMahon led his columns in person right up to the first houses, braving the concentrated fire poured from windows and rooftops. Most of the defenders were Croatian infantry who had already earned for themselves a sinister reputation as slaughterers of the wounded, and Tyrolean *Jaeger* battalions composed of picked marksmen.

'From then on,' says Zédé, 'all was confusion and chaos. The whole business degenerated into a series of savage encounters between small groups of men. I found myself in the principal street near Lieutenant-Colonel Martinez (commanding the 1st Foreign Legion Infantry Regiment) and my friend Giovaninelli; both of them were carrying rifles. Martinez' face was covered with blood – a bullet had shot away his left eyebrow – he was adjusting his *lorgnon* and ordered me to batter down a postern gate on his right. I pushed against it with my hand and called my men. The first to come running was the Drum Major, a giant who, picking up a heavy Tyrolean carbine lying on the ground, dealt the door such mighty blows that it was smashed in a matter of seconds.'

The corps' second division, commanded by General Espinasse, himself an ex-Legion officer, included both the 1st and 2nd Legion infantry regiments, and their war diaries state that the corps had converged on Magenta via Buscate and Marcallo. The nature of the ground made keeping contact extremely difficult. Towards midday the 2nd Brigade, which consisted of two Legion and a Zouave battalions, had taken up position in a brick factory to the right of Marcallo, the Zouaves in the centre, a Legion battalion on either flank. Suddenly the *Chasseurs à Cheval* who had been screening the advance began to fall back as heavy fire was poured into them from dense

Austrian columns, who then began to carry out an encircling movement.

The colonel of the 1st (Legion) regiment (says the war diary) with the company of *voltigeurs* commanded by Captain Rembert moved off to the west flank to intercept the Austrians and, deploying his men, opened fire at 100 metres range. The enemy was halted for a few moments but, vastly outnumbering us, began to move forward again. At that moment Colonel de Chabrière, commanding the 2nd regiment, a brilliant figure in his epauletted tunic, coolly sitting his charger, decided to intervene and gave the order – 'Off with your packs'.* Then, 'Forward the Legion'.

Levelling their bayonets the legionaries broke into the double; but because of the rough ground, ranks were broken and contact lost between the advancing companies. In spite of this, shouting '*En Avant*', they swept down on the Austrians like a tidal wave. Surprised, the enemy began to give way though still maintaining good order.

In vain Colonel Chabrière tried to regroup his regiment. He was carried along by the human current to the shouts of '*En Avant … En Avant*' till, an easy target on his plunging charger, he was killed outright by a well-aimed bullet. But such was the élan of the attack that the Austrians were pushed back to the railway embankment; that is to say that a good three kilometres had been covered by the enemy with Legion bayonets in their kidneys.

Just before the major assault on the town was launched, MacMahon, seeing the Legion regiments renewing their advance, clapped his hands and shouted, '*Voici la Légion. L'affaire est dans le sac!*' He anticipated. Victory would be his, but the 'affair' was not 'in the bag' till after a further eight long hours of ferocious combat.

The stolid, peasant-stock Austrian troops were at their best at street fighting. Told quite simply that there would be no retreat and no surrender, unconfused by complicated manoeuvring and muddled orders which, in any case, they often had difficulty in understanding, they did indeed carry out these sublimely simple instructions, in most cases preferring to die where they stood rather than throw down their arms. Every

---

* French infantry always carried excessively heavy packs. 'Down packs' was, therefore, a routine preliminary order before a charge.

house was a mini-fortress – Croatians on the lower floors, Tyroleans at the upper windows and on the roofs. Doors had to be battered down, shutters splintered. In solidly furnished rooms, across overturned tables, in the broken glass of fallen pictures and the relics of smashed ornaments, up and down narrow staircases, men fought it out with the bayonet.

Leading a platoon assault on a courtyard, General Espinasse and his ADC, Lieutenant de Froidefond, were killed, shot down at point-blank range. The last house was not stormed, the last shot not fired, till three o'clock on the morning of the 5th. A Zouave recalled that when at last the combat ended the survivors were too exhausted to sleep, but that luckily most houses boasted a cellar well stocked with *'un petit vin fruité qui enivre si agréablement'*. There were no arrests of those who found solace in being 'so pleasantly inebriated'. Instead the regiment was selected to be the first in the history of the French Army to receive a collective decoration. The standard of the 2nd Zouaves who had captured that of the 3rd Battalion of the Graf-Klarnstein Regiment was hung with the cross of the Legion of Honour. In the course of the same ceremony, a *cantinière*,* Antoinette Tremoneau, received the same award from the Emperor himself proof that, though France might be an empire, there was nothing undemocratic about the distribution of decorations.

Claimed as a great victory, Magenta was an indecisive action. Although all three armies had been in the area, no Piedmontese and roughly only one half the French and Austrians had been engaged. French losses were in the neighbourhood of two thousand killed and seriously wounded. Austrian casualties were considerably heavier, seven thousand being the figure generally quoted. Nevertheless, with the uncommitted troops under his command, Gyulai could well have stood his ground. Magenta was only a comparatively unimportant town – a milestone on the Milan road, admittedly,

---

* *Cantinières*, female camp-followers, were a time-honoured institution in the French army. Their duties varied from cooking, patching up uniforms, and rough care of the wounded to more intimate comforts. Many a young soldier was the son of a *'cantinière'* and of *'père inconnu'* ('father unknown').

but nothing more than a milestone.

The Austrian commander, however, did his country a final disservice by treating a minor tactical reverse as a major strategical disaster, by ordering the immediate evacuation of most of Lombardy, including the capital, Milan, and a stampeded retreat back across the Mincio to the Quadrilateral, a good hundred miles to the east. In every way the move was catastrophic. The evacuation of Lombardy constituted the gift of a morale and political victory out of all proportion to that won on the battlefield, and which was bound to have, as indeed it did, immense repercussions throughout the Italian peninsula and on the other European powers closely following the course of events. It was grossly unfair to inflict such a humiliation on men who had fought bravely and stubbornly, denying them either time to recuperate their physical forces before being spurred at a killing pace across the hot, dust-ridden plains, or the chance to strike back immediately, to wipe out the stigma of defeat.

Inevitably in the course of such a retreat there were stragglers, and the Lombard peasants, seeing the detested 'foreign oppressors' scuttling east in what gave the appearance of a near panic-stricken rout, did not hesitate to massacre them. Theirs indeed was the fate which, from time immemorial, has befallen those abandoned in the wake of a retreating army.

In Vienna, news of the loss of Lombardy was received with horror tempered at first by disbelief. It seemed impossible that a mighty army could, in the space of three weeks, have been not merely defeated but routed, by forces inferior in number and comprising a fair percentage of the same men who, only a decade previously, had themselves been so decisively crushed by Radetsky.

The shattering information reached Franz Josef at his headquarters in Verona as he was on his leisurely way to assume command. For him, too, incredulity mingled with dismay. Though there had been voices warning him that Gyulai was not the man to launch a *blitzkrieg*, he had preferred to listen to the counsel of his evil genius, Grunne. Now confronted by the result of his mistake, his immediate reaction was to prepare orders for Gyulai to halt his despicable retreat, turn about, and fight. He was dissuaded from so doing by his chief of staff, Field Marshal Hess, a man of great experience, who, though deploring Gyulai's flight, saw that to halt in the middle of so demoralizing a manoeuvre before having time to rest and regroup could prove even more calamitous. It was also vital, Hess urged, that Gyulai be dismissed forthwith, that Franz Josef take over command without delay and endeavour to efface in the shortest possible time the memory of such abysmal leadership – or, rather, lack of it. The Emperor concurred. Gyulai was peremptorily dismissed, and as from 17 June Franz Josef became the army's commander-in-chief.

Amazingly Gyulai did not seem the least perturbed, or show the slightest remorse at the enormity of his errors and the disasters they had entailed. Count Crenneville, the Adjutant-General, who carried the message of dismissal, was outraged, reporting that 'he (Gyulai) is in the best of spirits. He sees nothing wrong at all. He has all his comforts, good cooking, cards after dinner. He invited me to dine, but I excused myself ... this HQ turns my stomach and I could weep.'

Franz Josef was now faced by the agonizing question – what should be his first move? Hess remembered that Radetsky had gained his great victory over Charles Albert by luring him across the Mincio into the heart of the Quadrilateral. Yet this time the overall picture was very different. In 1848, before Custozza, the Austrian army was full of confidence in its own capabilities and in its leaders. Morale was high. Now, on the contrary, morale badly needed a substantial boost; confidence in themselves and in their commanders had to be restored.

The Quadrilateral was indeed an immensely strong position, but Hess was well aware that the best of defensive positions are no better than the men standing behind the ramparts, and in this case, suffering as they must be from a nagging inferiority complex, the only way in which the will to vanquish could be re-instilled was to switch over to the offensive, however costly such an offensive might prove to be. Franz Josef, however, was obsessed by the memory of 1848 and inclined to disagree with his chief of staff's theories on morale. Why not, he argued, force the allies to make the first move in the new situation which had evolved since Magenta? If the Austrians stood firm on the east bank of the Mincio, Victor Emmanuel and Napoleon would be obliged to attempt to force the passage against a mobile defence which, after inflicting maximum casualties on the attackers without being too deeply involved themselves, would then fall back, drawing the French and Piedmontese into the 'box' of the Quadrilateral. The one thing the allied army could not afford to do, Franz Josef stressed, was to stand still once the Mincio had been reached. If they did not feel themselves in sufficient strength to follow up initial successes, then supply difficulties, already rumoured to be giving cause for anxiety, would oblige them to turn about, thus leaving the Austrians time to bring up still further reinforcements prior to a re-invasion of Lombardy.

Several days were taken up with interminable staff conferences, but in the end it was Hess's ideas which prevailed. Possibly guilt-stricken, having seen at first hand the dismal results of not following tried professional advice, Franz Josef finally agreed that the Mincio should be recrossed and the offensive resumed at the earliest opportunity, an offensive which, Hess was quick to point out, had every chance of catching the enemy off balance.

For most of the battle of Magenta, Napoleon had set up an advanced headquarters near Buffalora bridge on the right bank of the river. It had been an anxious day. The uncertainty of the struggle matched his own uncertainty as to reactions in Paris should victory smile on the Austrians. So it was that when MacMahon's despatch rider burst into the HQ with the news that the last nest of enemy resistance had been overcome, and that the town was firmly in French hands, there was an explosion of joy.

Next morning, when MacMahon came to report in person, Napoleon went to meet him, embraced him and said warmly, 'I thank you for all you have done. I name you Marshal of France and Duke of Magenta.' A couple of hours later, the commander of the Imperial Guard, General Regnault de St-Jean d'Angely, was also raised to the dignity of Marshal. These promotions, however, were not to the liking of General Fleury, ADC and personal friend of Napoleon. In his memoirs he writes indignantly: 'The Emperor's generosity in according General MacMahon a marshal's baton was not justified. It was the Emperor himself and not his generals who was responsible for the victory. It was he who directed the battle and, by his presence in the most dangerous position between the Naviglio Grande and the half-destroyed bridge of Buffalora, inspired the Grenadiers and the Zouaves of the Guard with his own inflexible courage. Render unto Caesar the things that are Caesar's.'

Nevertheless, Napoleon was again a very worried man despite his momentary elation, when details of losses became known and the casualty list lengthened ominously. What would the widows, fatherless children and bereaved parents have to say when they learned the price that had been paid for a victory on foreign soil for a foreign cause which, they would probably argue, was no real French affair nor likely to affect the destiny of France? Nor was he indifferent to the coldness which had entered into his relations with Victor Emmanuel, reported to be so furious at having been 'kept out of the action' that he was thinking of cancelling the agreed overall command in favour of a dual direction of future operations, with the French and Piedmontese on an equal footing.

Differences were pushed to one side, however, when on 8 June, with a splendid outward show of unity, the allied army made its triumphal entry into Milan, the two monarchs riding side by side at its head, closely followed by the hero of the day, Marshal MacMahon, Duke of Magenta. There is a popular story that, in a supreme demagogic gesture, the newly created Marshal picked up a little girl and rode with her on his saddle through the streets lined by hysterically cheering crowds and beneath the tempest of flowers and petals cascading from balconies and windows.

The 2nd Legion war diary gives us a vivid, if somewhat naïve, picture of the scene: 'It was a glorious day for the entry of the French troops (no mention is made of the Piedmontese) in the Lombard capital. A joyous national though improvised fête for the Italians who, even the previous day, had still trembled under the detested Austrian yoke. But the day marking the birth of a new born nation was symbolized by the presence of the victors of Magenta. The legionaries were fêted everywhere. They found the girls pretty and were already getting a taste for Chianti and Asti.'

While Milan celebrated, Baraguey d'Hillier's 1st Corps had followed up the retreating Austrians, fighting a sharp rearguard action with troops who had not been involved on the 4th, at Melegnano. Though defeated and driven from the field, the Austrians fought so tenaciously, not hesitating to accept the most severe casualties, that Baraguey d'Hillier decided to call a halt to the pursuit. Thus, thanks to the rearguard's sacrifice, the main body of the Austrian army was able to make its way unharassed to the east of the Mincio.

Rather than allowing themselves the luxury of a halt and celebrations in Milan, the allies would have done better to press hard on the heels of the retreating Austrians as the first Napoleon undoubtedly would have done. Had they swept on after the Austrian rearguard had been virtually wiped out at Melegnano, they might have ended the war without having to fight another major battle. Magenta, it should be remembered, was captured in the early hours of 5 June. It was not till 17 June that Franz Josef took over from Gyulai. In the interim the Austrian army was virtually without a commander. Probably individual formations and units could have been relied on to resist a well co-ordinated offensive, but such resistance could, at best, have been merely sporadic.

During this time, Garibaldi had been fighting a little war of his own in the tumbled Alpine foothills forming the extreme left of the vague allied front, with his three thousand *Cacciatori Alpini* (Alpine *chasseurs*) whom he had helped to raise after Victor Emmanuel accepted the offer of his services. After his remarkable exploits in South America, and especially during the long siege of Montevideo when he and his famous 'red shirts' were the heart and soul of the defence, he had been supremely discouraged by his frigid reception by the revolutionary-hating Charles Albert in 1847. In 1849 he was involved in another famous defence, that of the Roman Republic against Marshal Oudinot's – eventually Marshal

Vaillant's – Mediterranean Expeditionary Force, fighting to restore the Pope to St Peter's. When the republicans collapsed, he had been able to escape to his native Nice and thence, back again, to the new world. He returned to Italy in 1857 to become vice-president of the Italian National Society, sometimes described as 'the secret instrument by which Cavour acted upon the different Italian States'. A confirmed patriot, in 1859 he immediately offered his services to Victor Emmanuel, who did not suffer from the prejudices which had consumed his father.

Nominated general, at the head of his three thousand officially designated a brigade, Garibaldi showed himself to be a master of guerrilla rather than 'set-piece' warfare.

His first major action was at Varese, a town whose inhabitants had themselves chased out the small enemy garrison but expected an hourly return in force. Though the town lay in a hollow and was backed by the two lakes, Lugano and Maggiore, in Garibaldi's opinion it lent itself to defence. The Austrians were back three days after they had been evicted, bumping into a hastily constructed perimeter thrown up by the *Cacciatori*. They were beaten off, leaving behind two hundred dead and thirty prisoners. When no further attack was launched the following day (27 May), Garibaldi decided to pass over to the offensive.

The Austrians were encountered in strongly entrenched positions on the heights round San Fermo village overlooking Lake Como. Though informers brought news that the enemy force numbered roughly nine thousand and was commanded by the very able General Urban, Garibaldi had no hesitation in attacking. San Fermo itself was captured and the surrounding heights were cleared at the cost of remarkably light casualties due to the intensive training of the *Cacciatori*, their mobility and high standard of marksmanship, and the self-reliance of each individual soldier on which Garibaldi insisted and which was to a great extent the secret of his success.

Shortly afterwards, however, appalling weather made it almost impossible to keep a close watch on enemy movements. Urban was able to regroup his badly shaken force, which he then split into three columns. One, acting as a bait, lured

Garibaldi into the Como, then withdrew after offering little resistance; the other, profiting by this diversion, slipped in behind the *Cacciatori* re-occupying Varese, only to be obliged to quit the town in a hurry when news came of Montebello, Palestro and Gyulai's precipitate retreat, leaving them dangerously isolated.

At the moment of the allied entry into Milan, Garibaldi was summoned to appear before Victor Emmanuel and warmly congratulated on his exploits. Back with his men the following day, he was off in hot pursuit of the retreating Austrians, occupying first Brescia then Lonato. He would have carried on had he not received a peremptory signal from the King ordering him to halt and wait for reinforcements. Victor Emmanuel had seen the danger. In Lonato Garibaldi was isolated, as the Austrians had been in Varese. Urban also realized this and made determined effort to turn the tables. With a greatly superior force he fell on two *Cacciatori* battalions which Garibaldi had moved to what he thought would be a much less vulnerable position at Trepanti.

The two battalions put up a determined resistance for three hours but were then forced to abandon the town, leaving behind a large number of dead and severely wounded. It was the first, and only reverse of the campaign.

Luckily for the Piedmontese, Urban did not follow up their retreat. His failure to do so gave Garibaldi time to re-organize. By 17 June he was again advancing and far ahead of the main allied army when he received further orders to swing south and back along the path he had already travelled, to block a possible Austrian move down the Valtellino Valley. It was while engaged on this mission that he heard of the victory at Solferino, and later of the Villafranca armistice.

One may find a parallel with this successful little campaign in the two Wingate expeditions in Burma in 1943 and 1944. It made no concrete contribution to final victory but, like the Wingate expeditions – and in particular that of 1943 – it was much publicized, bringing a touch of romance and high adventure to the otherwise grim business of war. It appealed to the civilian imagination more than did the course of the major operations, and at the same time won for Garibaldi an aura of superiority and a reputation confirmed as the most intrepid of all guerrilla leaders.

Only three weeks actually elapsed between Magenta and Solferino (24 June), but this allowed Franz Josef seven precious days in which to gather up the dropped reins. The Austrian army which met the Franco-Piedmontese in the greatest battle since Leipzig was, as a result, a cohesive entity. The delay, therefore, cost the allies a grim toll in lives which might well have been avoided. And for the Austrians, paradoxically, the fact that they were made a gift of these days to reform and regain much of their lost morale was equally tragic, for the result was defeat in any case. The mere fact that on 24 June they joined battle with sober hopes of victory, meant that many who might have survived surrender, albeit humiliating, after Magenta, perished on the hills and in the fields round Solferino, Cavriana and San Martino.

As Victor Emmanuel preferred to leave matters of policy to his Prime Minister, Cavour arrived in Milan on 9 June for talks with Napoleon. The talks opened in a strained atmosphere. Cavour did not really trust his interlocutor. He could not forget the hesitations which had driven him to contemplating suicide only a few weeks previously. It exasperated him to think that Piedmont's liberty of action was still largely dependent on French bayonets. As he had foreseen, early victories had produced immediate reactions in neighbouring Italian states. Already Tuscany had rid herself of the Grand Duke Leopold III, and it seemed likely that he would soon be followed into exile by the Duchess of Parma and Francis of Modena. Rome was again stirring. Above all Cavour was determined to extract from Napoleon that he would approve of Piedmont's immediate annexation of any state which rid itself of its foreign ruler. For him there was only one policy, one goal to be attained: unification – the creation of a united kingdom of Italy, whose royal house would be that of Savoy.

For Napoleon, on the other hand, the situation was infinitely more complex. He was desperately anxious to confine his commitments to the purely military sphere. The French army was in Italy to protect Piedmont from unprovoked Austrian aggression. Once the Austrian threat had been dealt with, it was up to the Piedmontese to put their own house in order. It certainly did not help that French troops were still in Rome. Their withdrawal and subsequent despoliation of the Pope – as it would seem to the strong Catholic element in France which included the Empress Eugénie – could well lose him an alarming number of his traditional supporters. He sympathized with Cavour but did not dare give the proposals his official blessing. Cavour, though bitterly disappointed by the Emperor's negative attitude, was level-headed enough not to say anything which might weaken Napoleon's avowed intention of 'liberating Italy from the Alps to the Adriatic'.

It was with a sigh of relief that Napoleon finally managed to persuade the Prime Minister that talks should be resumed at a later date and that now was the time to get on with winning the war. Talks, especially with a man of Cavour's dogged tenacity, exhausted him far more than a week in the saddle. Indeed as the allied army, now 200,000 strong, moved east towards the Mincio, he was happy to forget the tortuous world of politics and pray for a speedy and glorious victory, recalling his own words to the army just prior to Montebello – 'Soldiers! I have no need to stimulate your ardour; each stage of our march recalls a victory. On the sacred way of ancient Rome, inscriptions on the marble brought to mind great feats; so, today, as you pass by Mondovi, Marengo, Lodi, Castiglione, Arcola, Rivoli, you will be marching along another Sacred Way of glorious memories. I know that the new Army of Italy will prove worthy of her elder sister!'

The sweating Franco-Piedmontese columns plodded east under a blazing sun. On 21 June the Chiese river was crossed. A halt was then called for a rest after the gruelling march prior to deployment and the crossing of the Mincio, on whose eastern bank, both Victor Emmanuel and Napoleon were firmly convinced, the campaign's deciding battle would be fought. What neither they nor a single one of their senior commanders envisaged for a moment was the possibility of the Austrians launching an attack themselves, preceded by a crossing to the Mincio's west bank. And this was exactly what Hess had predicted.

It was during this halt that a revolutionary method of

reconnaissance was tried out. MacMahon was surprised to receive a visit from a man named Godard who explained that he was a balloonist, ordered to make an ascent to try to locate enemy positions. As all contact had been lost since Melegnano, the Marshal was delighted. The ascent was duly made in perfect weather, and on landing Godard reported that the area seemed clear of the enemy. The only movement he had spotted was a three-man cavalry patrol in the neighbourhood of Pozzolengo village to the south of Lake Garda. MacMahon, and later Napoleon, was of the opinion that this negative report confirmed their belief that no opposition would be encountered till the Mincio had been crossed.

8

Solferino: the Clash of Three Monarchs

The countryside separating the Chiese and the Mincio rivers did not present the nightmare, militarily speaking, so much a feature of that which had served as the setting for the battle of Magenta. It was undulating, the symmetry of its rolling slopes broken only occasionally by small, pimple-shaped hills. Hamlets and large individual farms were scattered over cultivated areas, with vineyards, orchards and corn fields. Visibility, generally, was excellent over the area where the battle would rage, a huge oblong, its north face the Lonato-Rivoltella-Peschiera road, the east the course of the Mincio from Peschiera to Mantua, the west a line parallel with the Chiese and passing through Castiglione, south an imaginary line from Asola to Mantua, below which spread the plain of Medole till abruptly halted by the foothills of the Apennines.

The Austrian soldiers knew the area well. It was a favourite venue for army manoeuvres, and to make the mock battles more realistic, the main heights had been covered with *ad hoc* fortifications and trenches. Tracks had been furrowed to slow the progress of make-believe enemy artillery. Thickets and hedges concealed well-sited gun positions.

Solferino village, from which the battle took its name, had also served in the past as the HQ of the staff directing the exercises. Equidistant between the Chiese and the Mincio rivers and the southern tip of Lake Garda, it was dominated by a medieval square tower, the Spia d'Italia, from whose summit the whole region could be kept under observation. At the western entrance to the village was a walled cemetery adjoining

the church of San Pietro, which the Austrians converted into a
bastion. To the right, separated from the village by a narrow
ravine, a rounded hummock planted with cyprus trees, the
Mont des Cyprées, commanded the unique track winding up to
the cemetery. This ensemble of village, tower, cemetery, the
Mont and the walled hamlet of Cavrianna formed the hub of
the Austrian line, the nerve centre of command, Franz Josef
setting up his battle HQ first in Solferino itself, then in
Cavriana.

On 22 June Napoleon and his staff were in Monte Chiaro
west of Castiglione, while Victor Emmanuel had halted west of
San Martino. Although the King still accepted the principle of
Napoleon as supreme commander, there is no record of an
overall plan having been worked out or of the presence of either
French or Piedmontese liaison officers on the respective staffs.
One has the impression that the advance and proposed
offensive were to be very much a 'playing it by ear' affair, at
any rate till the Mincio had been crossed and a substantial
bridgehead established on the east bank. Furthermore, it would
seem that neither Napoleon nor Victor Emmanuel took very
seriously the axiom that 'time spent in reconnaissance is seldom
wasted', though it is one that must have been firmly impressed
on the first Napoleon's mind and that of his marshals. When
the *Grande Armée* was on the move, the light cavalry was
always far ahead of the main body, its 'ears and eyes'. Thanks
to this highly mobile screen, every enemy move could usually be
anticipated and the following, slower-moving mass protected
against surprise. But on 23 June in the narrow strip between
the Chiese and the Mincio, the blindness – and deafness – of all
three armies was incredible. It is difficult to comprehend how
nearly half a million men could have ignored each other's
proximity for so many hours since by evening a bare two miles
separated their advanced posts. The only possible explanation
seems to be the extreme heat. After the freak rains of early
May, from mid-June all Europe was stifled by an equally freak
heatwave. London recorded 97 degrees in the shade. In
Lombardy the thermometer soared to well over one hundred.
All the tired troops wanted was a spot of shade for a prolonged
siesta, but even such extremes of weather were no valid excuse

for the negligence of commanders.

In the north Victor Emmanuel had halted, not intending to move till he received news that the French had begun their advance. His men were in bivouacs, as if on manoeuvres, such was his conviction that the Austrians were incapable of making any effort to regain the initiative.

To begin with, the French were not so complacent. On the afternoon of the 22nd, Baraguey d'Hillier ordered Commandant Morand's 1st Zouaves to occupy Solferino village. The French troops were welcomed enthusiastically by the *podestà* (mayor) and cheering villagers, thinking that their presence spelled a definite end to Austrian rule. That night the men, comfortably installed in billets, were soon sleeping soundly. Morand, however, was an habitually early riser. He was up before dawn and had settled himself in a point of vantage from which he would be able to survey the wide stretch of the river. As the horizon lightened, he could hardly believe his eyes. Columns of white-coated soldiers were swarming across a succession of bridges which seemed to have sprouted overnight. Substantial numbers were already established on the west bank. Recovering from the shock, Morand sent a runner hurrying back to Baraguey d'Hillier, who immediately ordered the Zouaves to pull back – much to the mayor's distress – and in turn sent a runner to inform Marshal Vaillant, the chief of staff.

This surprise intelligence could have precipitated the battle. Attacked as they were carrying out the crossing, the Austrians would have been highly vulnerable, but Marshal Vaillant, almost as if the mantle of Gyulai had fallen on his shoulders, did absolutely nothing. He did not even 'bother' to inform the Emperor, the supreme commander, and Baraguey d'Hillier, receiving no orders, was also quite happy to rest inactive once the Zouaves had been safely withdrawn, ignoring a desperate appeal from the mayor to re-occupy the village before such a naturally strong position could be seized by the enemy. Later Marshal Vaillant, who enjoyed the reputation of being a highly efficient, thoroughly professional officer, stated frankly that on receiving Morand's report he had discussed it with other members of the staff but had come to the conclusion that it was an exaggeration, that the enemy move could not be anything more than a reconnaissance in 'moderate' force, and that any unit that might have slipped across the river would soon pull back.

The Austrians showed no greater tactical flair than their opponents. Neither Franz Josef nor Hess suspected that the allies had advanced so rapidly that they were already across the Chiese, and this belief was encouraged by the fact that no opposition had been encountered during their own crossing of the Mincio. This success had taken a load off the Austrian Emperor's mind. He could not rid himself of the conviction that the best strategy to have been employed would have been that of Radetsky: luring the enemy into the Quadrilateral and letting it serve as a 'killing ground'. In the end he had yielded to Hess's cogent arguments chiefly because of the arrival of reinforcements and the news reaching him on the 21st of Prussian mobilization, leading him to hope that a victory such as Hess predicted would bring the Prussians into the war on a wave of pan-German sentiment.

So it was that on the night of the 23rd, thanks to this fantastic mixture of gross inefficiency and wishful thinking, Austrian, French and Piedmontese, slept blissfully unaware of what the morrow would hold.

Just before dawn on the 24th half a million men were stirring, grumbling at being woken so early, yawning, rubbing their eyes, checking equipment while coffee was brewed up, and chewing rancid ration biscuits. The scanty meal finished, if not digested, tents were folded, embers of camp fires stamped out, heavy packs heaved onto sore shoulders. Soon all three armies were on the move.

On the allies' extreme left, a Piedmontese brigade edged its way down the Lonato road. In the centre, Zouaves and the 2nd Foreign Legion formed the French advance guard probing east through swirling white mist preluding another blazingly hot day, while on a broad front, equally blindly, the whole Austrian army marched cautiously west.

Of these three armies soon to be locked in combat along a fifteen-kilometre front, the Piedmontese was much the weakest. Commanded by the King, with General La Marmora in the

ill-defined appointment of 'personal adviser', and General della
Rocca as chief-of-staff, it was made up of five infantry
divisions, commanded by Generals Durando, Fanti, Mollard,
Cialdini and Cucchiari, and a cavalry division under General
Bertone di Cambuy, in all some 55,000 men. The divisional
commanders took their orders direct from the King. Liaison
between them was non-existent. Rivalry between the respective
commanders was so acute that it was distressingly harmful
when it came to operating as a cohesive whole. The problem
posed by such a chain of command would have proved a severe
headache for the most gifted of staffs; for one as amateurish as
that of Victor Emmanuel, it was literally unsolvable, often with
calamitous results.

The French took the field with four corps and the corps of
the Imperial Guard, the same team which had prevailed at
Magenta, altogether a total of 173,603 men, including 14,553
cavalry and backed by an artillery train of 522 pieces.

On Hess's advice, Franz Josef split his force into two armies
for his counter-offensive. On his left was the 1st Army under
Feldzeugmeister von Wimpffen, comprising the 3rd, 9th and
11th Corps commanded respectively by Prince Edward von
Schwarzenberg, Field Marshal Count von Schaffgotsche and
Field Marshal Baron von Weigel (Veigl), and a cavalry division
under Count Medtwitz. The 2nd Army forming the right wing,
commanded by Count Schlick, was the stronger: four corps, the
1st, 5th, 7th and 8th, under Field Marshal von Benedek, Count
Stadion, Count Clam-Gallas and Baron von Zobel, and a
cavalry division commanded by Baron von Mensdorff – in all
146,653 infantry, 88 squadrons of cavalry and 688 guns.

Of these three armies the French was the most professional
and experienced. Men and commanders had fought in the
Crimea or in North Africa, or in both. The French were also
the best equipped. Their infantry rifle outranged that of the
Austrians, was lighter and more easily handled, while that of
the Piedmontese took no fewer than twenty separate
movements to load. French guns though inferior in number to
those of the Austrians, were of far better quality. Zédé, who
watched them being off-loaded at Genoa, described them as
'little bronze guns, very mobile, drawn by only four horses, still

muzzle loaded but with rifled barrels firing a cylindrical projectile whose accuracy and range was definitely superior to that of any other European army. As a result', he went on, 'we were about to start operations with both rifles and guns that we knew to be better than any possessed by the enemy. We didn't really need this knowledge to bolster our morale, which was very high, but it was comforting all the same.'

Because of the shocking blunders perpetrated by senior commanders both prior to and during the battle, Solferino has been described as a combat between 'lions led by asses'. Nobody can deny the enormity of the errors by leaders nor the stoic, outstanding courage and determination shown by the rank and file, yet in all fairness it should be pointed out that the 'asses' for the most part also displayed outstanding bravery as if striving to make amends for their mistakes.

Both Victor Emmanuel and Napoleon were fortunate to reach the end of the day unscathed. Both were frequently right up in the front line well within rifle range. If Franz Josef kept more aloof from the general mêlée, he too showed that he would not hesitate to risk his life, when he was one of the last to withdraw back across the Mincio. The general ineptness is, indeed, hard to understand on the other hand, for, unlike most of the British in the Crimea who had never heard a shot fired in anger, French and Piedmontese commanders were no strangers to the battlefield. General Durando, very much the revolutionary, had fought in Belgium and Portugal as a young man; Cucchiari had served against the Carlists in Spain; La Marmora and Cialdini had distinguished themselves at the Tchernaya battle in the Crimea. Later, when Savoy became part of France in 1860, Napoleon thought so highly of Mollard that he was offered immediate general's rank in the French army. In addition there was barely one senior officer present who had not seen service in the 1848 and 1849 campaigns.

On paper, the records of the French corps and divisional commanders could hardly have been more impressive. Though by then at the end of their long careers, Baraguey d'Hillier and Regnault de St-Jean d'Angely had been highly thought of by the first Napoleon. Apart from the Crimea, Niel, MacMahon and Canrobert were seasoned North African veterans. They were men who had steadily climbed promotion's ladder, knowing rules and regulations by heart, and the textbook answers to textbook situations. They were painstaking, reliable officers, normally to be counted on to do the right thing at the right moment, yet almost totally lacking in imagination – with the exception of Niel, lacking indeed that divine spark of genius without which no commander can hope to be qualified as 'great'.

The same could have been said of the majority of the divisional generals. Excellent routine soldiers, and notably Forey, Ladmirault, Bourbaki and Trochu, they did sterling work at Solferino, while, as has been seen, Forey had shown a momentary flash of genius at Montebello. Yet eleven years later their limitations were to be tragically exposed when France collapsed in the space of a few weeks before the onslaught of the Prussian military machine. Most junior of Baraguey d'Hillier's divisional commanders was Bazaine, doggedly working his way up the scale from trooper to Marshal, and showing himself progressively more incompetent with each ascending rung attained. How much better it would have been for him, for his reputation, for France, had he died that day at the head of his battalions!

Great personal courage combined with a spirit of self-sacrifice was also a characteristic of many of the senior Austrian officers, whose lack of military talent was comprehensible since high rank was largely a matter of social standing. Men like the gallant Karl von Windischgraetz and Prince Alexander of Hesse, the Czar's brother-in-law, commanded regiments simply because in Austria counts, barons, dukes and princes automatically assumed command whether or not they had had a suitable training or possessed the mental or physical equipment to fit them for such responsibilites. If a high-ranking Austrian officer did in fact prove himself capable, it was basically a matter of luck, as in the case of the Archduke Charles, always considered by the first Napoleon as one of his most dangerous opponents.

A notable exception was Field Marshal Ludwig von Benedek, of Hungarian origin. He embraced the military life at a very early age, not as an excuse to wear a gorgeous uniform but as a genuine profession whose apprenticeship, as he saw it, should be served under fire. He alone in 1859 had both talent and drive. At Solferino his 8th Corps outmanoeuvred and outfought the numerically superior Piedmontese army. Had he been commander-in-chief, 24 June might well have witnessed an Austrian victory.

One aspect is remarkable. At a time when longevity was an exception rather than a normality, most of the senior officers who survived Solferino lived to a ripe old age. MacMahon, Canrobert, von Hess, Cucchiari, Baraguey d'Hillier, Cialdini and the Emperor Franz Josef all lived to be well over eighty; Cucchiari, in fact, born in 1806, celebrated the birth of the twentieth century.

Thanks to allied inertia on the 23rd, by the time the sun was well up on the 24th, the Austrians enjoyed a distinct territorial advantage, having profited by the lack of opposition to their crossing of the river to occupy all the dominating high ground the length of the prospective battlefield including Pozzolengo, Solferino, Cavriana and Giudizzolo. Their artillery was already in battery and covering the approaches from the west. Nevertheless, when the first collisions occurred, they were as much taken by surprise as the allies.

In the central and southern sectors where the French were deployed, it was they who recovered first from the shock of finding themselves already at grips with the enemy. This may have been due not only to greater mental flexibility but also to generally better physical condition. The allies' commissariat was not of the highest order, but even if rations were meagre, at least a steady trickle did reach the front regularly, and coffee and biscuits had been available at the pre-dawn stand-to. But though the Austrian advance had not exceeded eight to ten miles at any point, it had far outstripped the supply services. Except for a lucky few who had brought with them a ration of fiery *eau-de-vie*, the Austrian soldiers went into battle on an empty stomach, making them particularly vulnerable to the grilling sun as the day wore on.

At seven o'clock, Napoleon, still at Monte Chiaro, had just finished dressing when Fleury burst in saying that a Captain d'Abzac had just arrived, having galloped all the way from MacMahon's HQ to report that the anticipated battle had already been joined. Not having been informed of Morand's experience of the previous day, the Emperor was incredulous; it could only be isolated detachments, he protested.

'No, Sire,' replied d'Abzac. 'It is the whole of the Austrian army. I have seen it for myself. It is deployed as far as the eye can see. Come yourself, Sire. You can hear the cannon.'

Napoleon was still disinclined to believe the agitated d'Abzac till ADCs sent by both Niel and Baraguey d'Hillier arrived with confirmation.

Realizing then that his intelligence staff had blundered badly, he ordered a calèche to be harnessed and, accompanied by Fleury and the Duke of Montebello, had himself driven at full gallop to Castiglione, his advance HQ, where he found his staff badly shaken and his special escort, the *Cent-Gardes*, drawn up in the village square.

After a brusque word of greeting, Napoleon jumped down from the calèche and climbed to the top of the church clock-tower from where he commanded a panoramic view of the countryside. In the words of one of his staff, it was one of those landscapes '*où se marient tous les luxes et toutes les puissances de la vegetation*' ('which combine all the profusion and all the powers of vegetation'), but at that moment Napoleon was not interested in nature's charms. On the contrary, he was horrified by the grave mistake that had been made in remaining idle throughout the previous day, rather than pushing forward so short a distance and seizing the hilltops now, as he could see only too plainly, held in strength by the Austrians. Only one course of action was feasible, he decided rapidly. The heights, and especially the centre with the village of Solferino, must be stormed even at the price of heavy casualties. If a hole were to be punched through what appeared to be the hinge of the widespread enemy line, the two wings might be separated with a consequent breakdown of cohesive command.

Hurrying down the winding stone stairs and out onto the square, he dismissed the calèche, mounted his favourite charger and, surrounded by the *Cent-Gardes*, the sun glistening on their breastplates, galloped in the direction of the firing, his intention to order an immediate assault by both the 1st and 2nd Corps on Solferino village. In the uncertainty which still dominated this very early stage, and the general ignorance as to the exact whereabouts of either friend or foe, his eagerness to get the planned attack under way brought him and his escort well within range of the Austrian infantry's rifles. He was right up with the leading companies of an Algerian *Tirailleur* battalion when his left epaulette was shot away and several of the *Cent-Gardes*, including their commander, Colonel Verly, were wounded. The Austrians were well aware that the horsemen in their gleaming breastplates were surrounding the person of the French Emperor and, as Hess freely admitted at a later date, concentrated their fire on the group in the hope that the death of the enemy commander-in-chief might create chaos.

The first senior officer Napoleon encountered was MacMahon. The Duke of Magenta was a badly worried man. The opening phase of the battle had convinced him that the Austrians enjoyed a strong advantage. Having won such renown less than three weeks previously, he was definitely anxious that his reputation should remain unsmirched. Caution rather than enthusiasm activated him. He pointed out to the Emperor that, if forced to give total support to Baraguey d'Hillier in the drive on Solferino, he must inevitably open up a dangerous gap between his own right and the left of General Niel's corps, which already, in his opinion, had pushed ahead too rapidly and was in danger of being cut off from the main body. Beside himself with impatience, Napoleon confirmed his orders, but to calm the Marshal's apprehensions he promised to close any gap that might be opened with the Guard, at the moment being held in reserve.

This he did with admirable promptitude. Just before eight o'clock, the Guard cavalry, commanded by General Morris, with the *Voltigeurs* in support, were ordered forward. The cavalry division was one of the world's most colourfully uniformed bodies, consisting of *Chasseurs*, *Guides*, Lancers, the Empress Eugénie's own regiment of Dragoons and *Cuirassiers*. As they cantered up to the firing line, they presented a picture which would have assured the success of any pageant. Grim reality, however, soon ousted the picturesque.

'Our 24 squadrons', Lieutenant Descharmes of the Empress's Dragoons noted in his diary, 'at the quick trot and canter raised such clouds of dust that it was not long before one became unrecognizable. As we passed through the lines of the artillery, men were standing on the limbers shouting to warn us of guns and wagons on our path into which we could have charged at any moment, and many of us were only saved by the incredible instinct of our horses throwing themselves right back on their hocks when they sensed an obstacle we and they were unable to discern ...' Nevertheless, by ten o'clock the whole division was in position, filling the widening gap between the 2nd and 4th Corps, while the *Voltigeurs* were held in readiness to be thrown into the main battle for the Austrian centre at the opportune moment.

Franz Josef had reason to feel quietly confident about the issue in this early phase. From the vantage point of his HQ installed in Solferino, he could see with his own eyes that the French attacks were ill co-ordinated, that Baraguey d'Hillier's and MacMahon's corps would be exposed to a withering fire from his massed artillery as they endeavoured to push home their assault uphill and across comparatively open ground. He noted the widening gap not only between MacMahon and Niel but also between Niel and Canrobert's 3rd Corps on the extreme right of the French line, for whereas Niel had pushed forward too impetuously, the cautious Canrobert was hanging back.

At this vital moment, however, when the Austrian Emperor's mind should have been crystal clear, with only one thought, one purpose, the winning of the battle, animating him, his brain was clouded after a sleepless night.

The reason for this near mental exhaustion was utterly mundane. For the ordinary citizen to be henpecked, tormented by matrimonial discord, is a tragedy for the individual concerned but hardly of general import even to his immediate neighbours; when a commander-in-chief is so tormented on the eve of a great battle, the consequences may be dire for the whole nation!

With her childish inability to see beyond the limited horizon of her personal whims and fancies, the young Empress Elizabeth had pestered, and still continued to pester, her husband to allow her to accompany him on the campaign. And as if these senseless pleas were not enough to distract him, Franz Josef's mother, the jealous Sophie, was at the same time bombarding him with complaints about his wife's mis-demeanours. It was only two days before the re-crossing of the Mincio that an even more petulant and reproachful letter than usual had been delivered to him, stating that, 'if she could not share the dangers of the battlefield' she washed her hands of all affairs of state. As far as she was concerned, 'it must be all or nothing'.

Distraught, distressed, Franz Josef pondered and brooded over this latest message. Unfortunately for him – and for Austria – he was not a man who could brush such matters aside, dispassionately, good humouredly or even impatiently. All through the night of the 23rd he sat up miserably, straining his eyes by the light of a single candle, composing a letter which he prayed would open his wife's eyes to the true facts of the situation, at the same time awakening in her some understanding of her duties as Empress:

My dear, dear, only Angel (he wrote), I beg you in the name of the love you have sworn me, try to take hold of yourself, show yourself sometimes in the city, visit the hospitals and institutions. You simply do not realize how much help that would be to me. It would encourage the Viennese and raise their morale which is so important. Alas I cannot grant your desire to join me though it would please me so much if I could. Women simply do not fit into the life of a military headquarters. I cannot set a bad example to my whole army – and moreover it is impossible to say how long I may be here. Please my angel if you love me do not torment yourself so much.

Though, like Magenta, Solferino soon developed into a 'soldiers' battle', there were many instances when a rapid decision, a clear vision, that fractional anticipation of enemy intentions, might have tipped the scales. But in the mental state in which Franz Josef found himself on the morning of the 24th, the power to seize a presented occasion by that marginal thread on which may hang either triumph or disaster was totally absent. Above all he should have concentrated on Niel's comparative isolation, so clearly visible, to have ordered a devastating attack by von Wimpffen's 1st Army to annihilate the French 4th Corps before either MacMahon, heavily engaged in the centre, or Canrobert, far to the rear on the right flank, could have had time to intervene. He did not. And by failing to seize this unique opportunity, he gave the French time to recover from their initial surprise and to exploit their greater flexibility and flair for improvisation.

By ten o'clock the battle had broken up into four separate encounters, but, nevertheless, the crisis was approaching. In the north the whole Piedmontese army was being hurled in a series of generally unsuccessful assaults on Benedek's 8th Corps. Baraguey d'Hillier was preparing to launch an attack on Solferino village but was delayed by MacMahon, held up by the defences on Cavriana ridge, not giving him the support anticipated. Niel, to the south and far ahead, was being hard pressed but not hard enough to give him any serious concern, while, to the extreme right of the French line, Canrobert remained more or less static. From Napoleon's point of view, the situation was far from satisfactory, for the splitting up of the front was delaying the massive concentration he had hoped would result in the destruction of the Austrian centre.

Towards eleven o'clock, Baraguey d'Hillier seemed to be making real progress. Showing a sublime courage, a true *furia francese*, de Ladmirault's division had launched a series of frontal attacks and despite heavy losses overrun the lower slopes and pimple-like hillocks to the north of Solferino village, but was then halted by well-sited positions on the Mont des Cyprées. The infantry tried to work their way through the ravines and miniature valleys separating the shrub-covered hills, only to find them enfiladed, veritable death traps. By midday the division was truly pinned down; the men were worn out, hungry, thirsty, drenched in sweat: the sun was so fierce that many were on the verge of heat exhaustion.

The fighting had been of almost unparalleled ferocity. It was as if passions exacerbated by the heat had turned each individual soldier into a veritable homicidal maniac.

> The serried ranks hurled themselves at each other with the impetuosity of a mountain torrent sweeping everything before it. The French regiments deployed in open order were locked in combat with the Austrian masses which resembled iron ramparts.
>
> Whole divisions downed their packs so as to have all the more freedom of movement to charge with the bayonet.
>
> A battalion is hurled back, another takes its place.
>
> Every hillock, every height, every rocky ridge is the theatre of desperate combats ...

This picture of the battle portrayed by the Swiss observer Henri Dunant in his *Un souvenir de Solferino* was to stay with him all his life.

> Austrians and allies trampled one another under foot, slaughtered each other on a carpet of bloody corpses, smashed each other with rifle butts, crushed each other's skulls, disembowelled each other with sabre or bayonet.
>
> It was butchery; a battle between wild beasts maddened and drunk with blood.
>
> Even the wounded fought to their last breath.
>
> A man disarmed grappled with his enemy trying to tear out his throat with his teeth.

Napoleon, who, whatever his detractors may say, was essentially a compassionate man, acutely sensitive to human suffering, on the day of Solferino seemed possessed of a furious energy the like of which he was never to display again. Seeing that the 1st Corps' assault was pinned down, he ordered one of his most precious regiments, the *Voltigeurs* of the Guard, to pass through Ladmirault's exhausted battalions to renew the attacks on the summits, concentrating on the Mont des Cyprées.

A flamboyant scene worthy of an *image d'Epinal* followed on this order. The *Voltigeurs* had been straining at the leash, eager to prove themselves truly the élite. As their columns filed past Napoleon, their shouts of '*Vive l'Empereur*' almost drowned the roar of battle; the famous uncle might well have been smiling happily in his new resting place in Les Invalides.

No sooner had the *Voltigeurs* moved up preparatory to the assault than they had to meet a violent counter-attack by infantry of Stadion's 5th Corps. After fierce hand-to-hand fighting it was thrown back, and the *Voltigeurs*, reinforced by a regiment of the *Chasseurs* of the Guard, resumed their advance. Ladmirault's division, now slightly rested and joined by that of Forey, was then pivoted to the Guard's left flank. By now, too, most of 2 Corps was fully committed to the task of storming the Austrian centre.

Each hill, each pimple, was stubbornly defended. The one thing the Austrian soldier did not lack was courage, but on both sides that spirit of chivalry momentarily manifest at Palestro was missing. 'The Zouaves', one reads, 'hurled themselves forward, bayonets levelled, shouting and leaping like animals ... the general fury was such that when ammunition ran out and rifles were broken, men fought with bare hands ... the Croatians killed everything in sight and bayoneted their wounded enemies ... the Algerian *Tirailleurs*, howling like wolves, cut the throats even of the dying.' Nor was this blood lust confined to the infantry. In the plain, where a furious action developed between Austrian Uhlans and French Hussars, 'even the horses, excited by the bloody inebriation, attacked each other, ripping at each other with their teeth'.

When the first waves of *Voltigeurs* and *Chasseurs* had fought their way almost to the crests of the hills and ridges under an intense and accurate fire, they were again halted by well-sited, solidly constructed defences thrown up the previous day, most of them concealed by folds in the ground and therefore immune from the fire of French artillery on the lower slopes. Realizing that these defences must be overrun if the attack were to be pressed home with any hope of success, a battalion of *Voltigeurs* and *Chasseurs* laid down their rifles and, acting as coolies, hauled the guns uphill to within point-blank range of their targets. Many of them and the gun crews were mowed down, but a couple of salvoes were enough to demolish the ramparts and allow the Guards to fight their way in with the bayonet. Resistance was fierce, the Guards' casualties were high, but within half an hour the Mont des Cyprées had been cleared, Colonel d'Auvergne of the *Voltigeurs* tying his huge red handkerchief to the branch of a tree to signal this local victory.

Senior officers had suffered heavily. General Forey was badly wounded in the hip, two of his ADCs had been killed, one of them, a Captain de Kervenoel, having had the top of his head blown off by a shell. General Dieu had fallen at the head of the *Voltigeurs*. Though his left arm was smashed to pulp by shrapnel, Brigadier-General Auger of Forey's division refused to leave the field. He was promoted Major-General on the spot and killed a few minutes later. General de Ladmirault's left shoulder was fractured by a bullet. He had the wound bandaged then hurried back to the forefront of the battle, only to be wounded in the left leg within a few seconds.

The Mont des Cyprées firmly in French hands, the attack on Solferino village was renewed, Napoleon again right up in the firing line, extremely lucky to be untouched and showing, despite his fifty-one years, a remarkable indifference to the Saharan heat. As at Magenta, every one of Solferino's houses had been converted into a miniature fortress, while the cemetery of San Pietro, held by two Croatian battalions, was a veritable bastion which had been holding out for four hours against repeated attacks by the 2nd Foreign Legion. In one of these attacks, a Legion officer, who was always accompanied by his dog, a huge rangy mongrel, was killed by a bullet in the heart. A few seconds later the dog was also hit but 'the faithful animal was just able to summon up the strength to crawl back and die stretched out across the body of his master'.

The struggle for Solferino, the surrounding hamlets and Cavriana was reaching its climax with the waves of the French assault smashing on, then recoiling from the rock of the Austrian defence. Yet after each momentary repulse, the French infantry reformed to charge again. For some it was a heady experience, as one young lieutenant admitted after the battle. The smell of powder, the cannons' roar, the beating of drums and the bugles sounding, set his pulse racing madly – '*Ça vous anime*,' he said. '*Ça vous excite*.' ('It exhilarates you. It excites you.')

At last, by two o'clock in the afternoon, Solferino was in French hands, the Emperor Franz Josef driven from his headquarters. Scenes of incredible bravery had been witnessed before the last bullet ricocheted in the narrow alleys. Colonel de

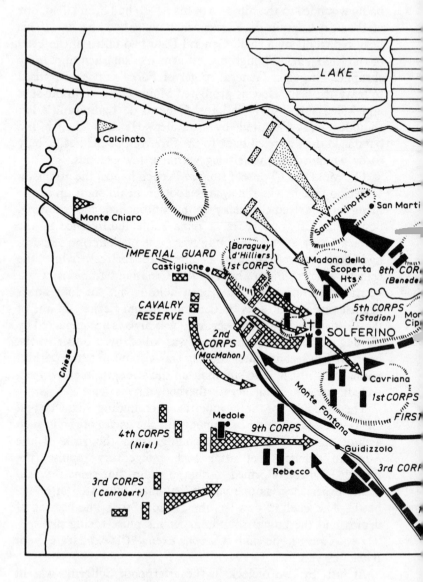

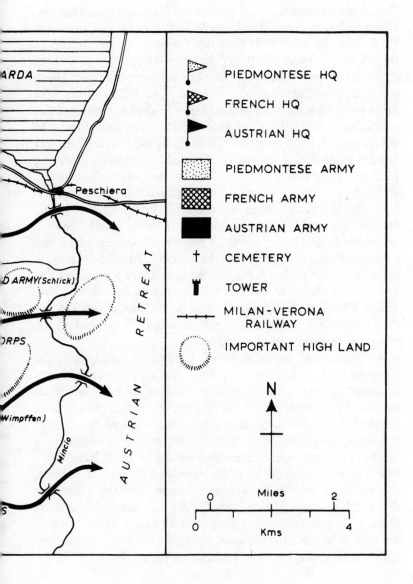

PIEDMONTESE HQ

FRENCH HQ

AUSTRIAN HQ

PIEDMONTESE ARMY

FRENCH ARMY

AUSTRIAN ARMY

✝   CEMETERY

TOWER

MILAN–VERONA
RAILWAY

IMPORTANT HIGH LAND

N

Miles

Kms

Malleville, commanding the 55th Regiment of the Line, was informed that his ammunition was exhausted. Seizing the Regimental standard, he galloped to the forefront shouting, '*Qui aime son drapeau me suive. Allons les braves du 55ème. En avant!*. ('Who loves his standard follow me. Come on my gallant lads of the 55th. Forward!) A bullet smashed his right leg, but he managed to stay in the saddle till the Austrian position had been stormed at the point of the bayonet. The following day the damaged leg was amputated. De Malleville died as a result of this operation carried out without anaesthetic. Pushing ahead into the village square, Lieutenant de Guiseul, standard-bearer of another line regiment, found himself surrounded by Austrians emerging from side streets. Mortally wounded by their first volley, he fell, clutching the flag to his chest. A sergeant raced forward to save it from the enemy; his head was shot off. In turn the company commander tried to raise the standard from the ground and fell 'dyeing its folds with his blood'. It was not till protected by a 'last rampart of dead and dying' that the rest of the battalion arrived to drive the Austrians back. Houses changed hands several times as attack was followed by counter-attack, then by counter-counter-attack. Five times the Foreign Legion battled its way into the San Pietro cemetery to be thrown out as often till the last of the Croatian defenders was bayoneted.

As the defence began to waver, Lieutenant Maniglia of the *Chasseurs* of the Guard captured six guns, four of them limbered up, the artillery colonel handing him his sword on surrendering. From the village church, which had been heavily fortified, the *Chasseurs* captured the standard of the Gustav von Wasa Regiment of Grenadiers, the regiment which for a brief period had been commanded by the Duke of Reichstadt, 'the *Eaglet*', son of the first Napoleon and his second empress, the Austrian Archduchess Marie Louise, shortly before his death. On that day of Solferino, the division to which the Wasa Grenadiers belonged was commanded by Count Monte Nuovo, another of Marie Louise's sons, whose father was the one-eyed Count Adam von Neipperg, for many years her lover.*

---

* It had been thought tactful to give the young Neipperg the Italian version of his name. One may compare the anglicization of the name Battenberg to Mountbatten.

The taking of Solferino was a marked success, but Napoleon was determined there should be no let-up until the entire enemy centre had been driven in. After Solferino, therefore, the next major objective was Monte Fontana. The position fell to the Algerian *Tirailleurs* after repeated bayonet charges. Again losses were heavy, including two battalion commanders, Colonels Laure and Herminet, both victims of Tyrolean marksmanship.

The last of the central strongpoints to be overrun was Cavriana Ridge. In this action the Guards artillery played a major role. Napoleon, like his uncle, had made his military début as a gunner. It was thanks to his interest in this arm that the French possessed the most modern guns of any European army. Before the infantry was ordered to move forward, Napoleon took temporary command of the artillery, personally checking the laying of every gun before fire was opened. The result, for the day, was devastating. The over-crowded defenders were decimated, their positions reduced to rubble; it was a frightening preview of things to come. When the infantry advanced, they were able to storm the crest with comparatively slight losses, while the Austrian retreat savoured of a rout, some of the units streaming back out of control towards the Mincio bridges.

Though his centre had fallen, splitting his forces in two, Franz Josef still had a chance of turning the day if not into a victory at least into a stalemate. His losses had been heavier than those of the French. A number of high-ranking officers lay dead on the field, among them Baron von Sturmfeder and Baron Plidoll; de Crenneville, who had been so disgusted by Gyulai's complacency after defeat, and General Palffy, one of Count Stadion's divisional commanders, were severely wounded. Yet the situation was not as hopeless as might have been imagined at first sight.

Despite the fact that the centre had collapsed, operations were developing far from unsatisfactorily on either flank. In the north Benedek was having little difficulty in beating off Piedmontese attacks and believed that he could soon switch over to the offensive. In the south, after seizing Medole, Niel's original onrush had been halted dead by superior forces leaving him in a precarious position since neither MacMahon, himself heavily engaged, nor Canrobert, only with some difficulty maintaining his ground, could come to his assistance. Indeed, Canrobert was under a serious threat of annihilation, being heavily attacked by fresh troops just arrived from Mantua under Prince Edward of Lichtenstein, and von Weigel's 11th Corps.

Till the afternoon the Austrians had failed to take advantage of the opportunities offered them. Co-operation between the 1st Army commander von Wimpffen and his corps was extremely poor. The concentrated efforts of Schaffgotsche, Schwarzenberg and Weigel could have overwhelmed Niel, after which nothing could have prevented Canrobert from suffering a similar fate. Instead the Austrians had been hammering away at both the French corps simultaneously, throwing in unco-ordinated attacks seemingly at the whim of divisional commanders, which proved not only futile but costly.

It was only after the fall of Solferino and the establishment of a new battle headquarters on a shrub-covered hill halfway between Solferino and the Mincio, that Franz Josef issued directions which, had they been given out earlier in the day, might have had a decisive effect on the final outcome. Von Wimpffen was instructed to hold both Niel and Canrobert with minimum forces, then, concentrating the bulk of all three corps (3rd, 9th and 11th), smash through the gap between Niel and MacMahon as far as Castiglione. From there, swinging in a vast encircling movement, he was to fall on the rear of the Imperial Guard, Baraguey d'Hillier and MacMahon, at the same time Schlick's 1st and 7th Corps redoubled their frontal attacks from the north, thus crushing their adversaries in a hammer-and-anvil operation.

Unfortunately for the Austrian cause, these orders reached von Wimpffen at least three hours too late and, in addition, once received were ineptly executed. Wimpffen was not a Gyulai, but he lacked the energy, the drive and the personal charisma to spur his subordinate officers and his men to make the supreme efforts necessary to achieve success at so late a stage.

In the meantime, what remained for most of the day an

entirely separate battle was being contested furiously on the extreme left (north) of the allied line.

From the moment the eastward march was resumed after the Milan victory celebrations, Victor Emmanuel, still smarting from the alleged affront of Magenta, was determined that the Piedmontese must outshine their French rivals the very next time the enemy were encountered. Had he not been so impatient, some effort might have been made to improve the cumbersome command system making effective central control so impossible a task. As it was, on the evening of the 23rd della Rocca issued vague instructions to each of the divisional commanders to cross the Mincio between Peschiera and Salione, seek out the enemy and destroy him.

Before dawn on the 24th, the five infantry divisions – the cavalry being held in reserve instead of employed in a reconnaissance role – set out, preceded by a small vanguard, without having made any attempt to establish even the most basic intercommunication network, and completely out of touch with army headquarters.

Benedek, on the other hand, though not informed of the Piedmontese advance, was expecting it. So it was that, when the leading elements of the Piedmontese 3rd and 5th divisions groping their way forward came under fire, they soon discovered that they had not bumped into equally blindly groping Austrian patrols but carefully prepared positions from which they were pushed back in some disorder after being very roughly handled. And since they were out of touch with neighbouring formations and feared being outflanked, the momentary retreat occasioned by this rude surprise was carried on too far, allowing Benedek to occupy the key position of the San Martino heights with a force of eight battalions and sixty-two pieces of artillery by eight o'clock in the morning.

A little to the south, the main body of General Filiberto Mollard's 3rd division was more successful. His 'Cuneo' brigade, under Major-General Arnaldi, ran into the Austrians in the region of Madonna della Scoperta. After a brisk action, Arnaldi penetrated into the centre of nearby San Martino village, captured a large farmhouse and its outbuildings, known as the Contracania, and a small rocky eminence between the farmhouse and the village. Benedek reacted vigorously. Personally leading the counter-attack, he drove the Piedmontese from all three positions after fierce hand-to-hand fighting during the course of which Arnaldi was seriously wounded.

Having regained the three key points, Benedek made no attempt to pursue the badly shaken 'Cuneo' brigade. The brigade, he judged, was probably the leading formation of the whole of the Piedmontese army. Instead, he ordered that the heights, the village and the immediate neighbourhood be converted into a solid defensive line against which, he calculated, the brave but poorly led Piedmontese would hurl themselves in a series of ill-planned counter-attacks, thus contributing to their own destruction.

His reckoning was sound, yet one feels that a little boldness, the willingness to take a risk in exploiting an initial advantage profiting by his enemy's momentary disarray, might have resulted in the complete disruption of the scattered Piedmontese and the turning of the French left flank before the latter's assaults on the Austrian centre had been crowned with success.

The Piedmontese 1st and 2nd divisions now arrived on the scene, and a combined attack by twelve battalions regained a number of the Contracania outhouses, only to be thrown out again 'in some confusion' by the inevitable Austrian counter-attack. General Fanti, however, managed to regroup his 2nd Division and turned his attention to Madonna della Scoperta, which he was able to storm almost unopposed, Benedek having already withdrawn most of the holding troops to a more advantageous position on a nearby dominating ridge.

In the meanwhile the glaring inefficiency of the Piedmontese command was again exposed when both Mollard's 3rd Division and Cucchiari's 5th were faced by the task of carrying the San Martino heights. Neither general could swallow his pride and agree to the other assuming temporary command of the combined divisions so as the better to co-ordinate the assault. Neither thought of trying to contact army headquarters to obtain a ruling on the question, nor was there any GHQ liaison officer on the spot who might have settled the problem. Each of the two divisions, therefore, staged its own independent attack, making no attempt to synchronize timing, giving no mutual support and without even coming to a decision as to individual objectives. As was only to be expected, the ragged assaults were bloodily repulsed by the well-entrenched Austrians.

Then, after these setbacks, Cucchiari, whose division had been continually in action since daybreak and whose men were showing signs of hyper-fatigue and collapsing morale, suddenly pulled back to Rivoltella without a word of warning, leaving the 3rd Division out on a limb and the artillery of both divisions without protection in the case of an enemy renewal of his advance.

That Benedek failed to take advantage of Cucchiari's thoughtless withdrawal was due to the growing exhaustion of his own troops, worn out by ceaseless combat and exposure to the merciless sun. Nevertheless, he had every reason to feel satisfied at the course of events. His single corps had, for the best part of nine hours, defied the efforts of the entire Piedmontese army from the dominating position he had won in the opening phase. Compared with those of the enemy, his losses had been light, and whereas the Piedmontese were beginning to show the unmistakeable signs of battle-weariness, his own troops were still full of confidence.

Finding himself abandoned, Mollard sent a Captain Edouardo Driguet, later Lieutenant-General, to find the commander-in-chief and inform him of Cucchiari's action. After a long and hazardous search, Driguet eventually discovered the King standing in the open in full view of the enemy. He was alone. His staff was sheltering out of sight, profiting from the cover afforded by a reverse slope.

Told of Cucchiari's flight and the failure of the attacks on San Martino, Victor Emmanuel, Driguet says, completely lost his temper. 'That damn'd Cucchiari,' he shouted. 'Another of *them*.' He gestured in the direction of the slope and his hidden staff: 'Just like the rest of that bunch, cowering from the cannon like a lot of ships skulking in harbour and not daring to put to sea.'

Driguet, however, had not gauged the full depth of his bitterness. As the King watched the French advance and saw the French flag flying over Solferino, Cavour's words, '*Guai a noi si devremo la nostra independenza ai francesi*' ('Woe betide us if we have to owe our independence to the French'), were ringing in his ears. The thought that Solferino should prove an even greater reproach to national pride than Magenta was intolerable, for whereas the Piedmontese had not been present at the latter battle, this time the French would be justified in boasting that they were winning *in spite of* their allies!

In desperation he ordered La Marmora, who till then had been playing the completely negative role of 'Adviser to the C-in-C', to mass four divisions for a final assault on San Martino and to wrest '*a qualunque costa la posizione al nemico*' ('the position from the enemy no matter what the cost'). Such a concentration might have succeeded, but at the last moment La Marmora made the elementary mistake of weakening the blow by sending one of the divisions to execute a diversionary attack on Pozzolengo, with the result that once more the Piedmontese were driven back, losing heavily and not having made the slightest impression on the Austrian line. Only one positive result was obtained, but neither the enraged Victor Emmanuel nor the contrite La Marmora knew of it till some weeks later. Seeing himself so violently assailed, Benedek felt obliged to ignore an urgent request from Franz Josef to send his corps to relieve the pressure in the centre.

It was at the moment that the defeated Piedmontese were straggling back, between 4.30 and 5 p.m., that a violent storm of unprecedented fury burst over the battlefield, paralysing operations for over an hour.

While in the centre the French were frantically digging in, preparing for the inevitable counter-attack, the main scene of action switched to von Wimpffen's massive attempt to break through to Castiglione. Observing the sudden enemy concentration, Napoleon sent an ADC to Canrobert's HQ, warning him that it looked as though Niel was about to be assailed by a considerably superior force, and urging that in the case of a crisis every help be given, advising him at the same time to keep a sharp watch on his own right flank should the corps from Mantua, in turn, attempt a wide outflanking movement to the south. Pressure was in fact soon brought to bear on the 3rd Corps, especially on that open right flank. In the words of one of Canrobert's staff, 'All around us shells were performing their deadly dance on the ground where the stricken vegetation was flattened like the men who had fallen, broken like those sleeping the sleep of death. Invisible but noisy aerial visitors, bullets whistled past our ears; sometimes striking branches which snapped off with a dry crack; sometimes men and horses who fell silently.'

These attacks, were, however, diversionary, easily repulsed by General Trochu's infantry* and General Partonneaux's cavalry who, spreading out into the plain, blocked an attempt by the Prince of Lichtenstein to turn the flank.

The main weight of von Wimpffen's blow fell on the cavalry of the Guard, reinforced by the 2nd Corps' Hussars and *Chasseurs d'Afrique* covering the gap between the 2nd and 4th Corps. To begin with, the Austrians met with a measure of success, the Guards in particular being extremely roughly handled by von Mensdorff's squadrons. Only the prompt intervention of General Soleille, commanding the Guards' artillery, in concentrating forty-two guns wheel to wheel, thus repeating Marshal Macdonald's decisive manoeuvre at Wagram, prevented a clean breakthrough. The Austrian infantry followed up the horsemen, then ran into the same withering fire and, as they wavered, were charged by the French cavalry, who had quickly reformed.

At the same time, General de Failly's division, the left wing of Niel's corps, was under extremely heavy attack from the Khevenhuller-Metsch Regiment, led by one of the most popular officers of the whole Austrian army, Prince Karl von Windischgraetz, whose initial blow fell on the 76th of the Line and a battalion of *Chasseurs à Pied*. The Prince's bravery was suicidal. A conspicuous figure in his gorgeous uniform, well ahead of the leading files, he was hit in the chest. Summoning his fast-draining strength, he managed to remain in the saddle till a dozen of his men, seeing him sway, ran to his aid. With his

---

* At the moment that the 3rd Republic was proclaimed in 1870, Trochu, supposed to be responsible for the safety of the Empress Eugénie, went over to the republicans.

last breath he was able to order that, like El Cid's, his dead body should be held upright in the saddle to act as a standard every man in the regiment would follow. It was only when his terrified charger panicked and plunged through the ranks that his body crashed to the ground. Dismayed at the loss of an adored leader, the regiment faltered, was violently counter-attacked, then scattered, leaving a battalion flag in the hands of Private Dreyer of the *Chasseurs*.

At Monte Fontana, so hardly and so dearly won, the Algerian *Tirailleurs* and the 70th of the Line of General Decaen's division (2nd Corps), were dislodged from their gains by a column led by Prince Alexander of Hesse. For the second time it seemed as if the road to Castiglione might be opened, but the Algerians, more at home under the gruelling sun recalling their native Sahara than the Europeans, recovered remarkably quickly from the shock and closely followed by the 70th turned on the Austrians in a wild bayonet charge. As the packed ranks grappled, thrust, hacked at each other, victory hanging in the balance, the *Voltigeurs* of the Guard came charging down from Cavriana Ridge to crash headlong into the Austrian left flank.

Von Wimpffen's counter-offensive had been checked at every move, but in general his men had not lost heart. Certain that the French, who had done most of the attacking throughout the day, must be suffering from severe strain, Franz Josef sent an ADC galloping to the 1st Army commander's HQ with orders to renew his assault at the first possible opportunity. The French, the Emperor insisted, had been within an inch of breaking; one more determined effort and Magenta would be avenged.

That fatal lack of discipline, so much a feature of the higher echelons in the imperial Austrian army, now made itself disastrously apparent.

Von Wimpffen, profoundly discouraged by the repulse of his initial blow, chose to turn a deaf ear to his instructions. Without consulting imperial HQ or giving any warning of his intentions, he ordered that all contact with the enemy be broken off and that his whole army fall back to the Mincio bridges and thence across to the east bank. Later taken to task, but surprisingly not placed under arrest for such flagrant disobedience at so critical a moment, he defended himself vigorously. He denied that most of his men were still full of fight. Quite the contrary, he argued, they were dropping with fatigue, hunger and thirst, approaching total demoralization, a result of their stubborn defence and equally courageous offensive's failure. He could ask no more of them. It was only by his action, he asserted, that the army was saved from annihilation, so that, once the withdrawal had been carried out, it still remained such a formidable fighting force that the French Emperor had been happy to conclude an armistice.

There may have been an element of truth in von Wimpffen's apologia, for, powerless to halt this retrograde movement, Franz Josef could only admit the battle lost and abandon the field to his allies, his one aim to get as many of his men as possible safely to the Mincio's east bank, there to regroup, and gamble on the possibility of being able to put into force his original plan to emulate Radetsky.

Nevertheless, he was overcome by chagrin. One of his staff recounted later that, as he was issuing instructions confirming the general retreat, tears streamed down his cheeks.

It was now the turn of the French to let slip the occasion to inflict total, crushing defeat on their opponents. It needed very little to convert the retreat into a panic-stricken flight, for, though most of the Austrian units maintained good discipline during the withdrawal, there were some, notably Hungarians and frontier Italians, who had little wish to die for an Emperor whose tongue they could barely understand and who, losing all sense of order, broke their ranks in a stampede to be the first to arrive at the bridges − 'In vain their officers who had fought like lions tried to control them; pleas, exhortations, blows with the flat of a sabre, nothing could stop them.'

Unable to rally the fugitives, many Austrian officers preferred to stand their ground alone and fight on till killed rather than join in the retreat. Others were so shamed that they committed suicide by throwing themselves onto the points of their swords. At one moment it seemed as if Franz Josef had lost all semblance of self-control. His despair, it was said, was immeasurable. He who had borne himself like a hero, who had seen bullets and shells rain down about his person, spurred forward, wild with grief, to the head of the fugitives and curse them for their cowardice.

Only on regaining his calm after this legitimate lapse, and after casting about him a last mournful look over this fateful field of carnage and on the urgent pleas of his *aides-de-camp*, did he agree to leave Volta for Valeggio.*

At 5 p.m. Fortune, in the guise of the weather, decided at last to smile on the Austrians. Black clouds had been rolling up on the horizon for the last half hour; then, accompanied by a wind of near tornado force, a storm like the arrival of the Bengal monsoon burst over the battlefield, drenching, torrential rain, hail; terrifying lightning flashed the roar of thunder drowning that of the cannon. And like the unleashing of the monsoon which transforms dusty paddy fields to spongy swamps in a matter of minutes, the storm converted the dustbowl of the Solferino arena into a gluey quagmire, bringing movement of any kind to a virtual standstill.

Ploughing through the mud, Austrian infantry, cavalry, artillery struggled back to the Mincio bridges. The gap between the two armies so recently interlocked in deadly combat widened as no pursuit order was forthcoming from the French command. The blood lust that had gripped men like a contagious disease gave way to an almost childish delight in being soaked under the deluge. Instead of hounding the momentarily demoralized Austrians, the French seemed to forget about the business of killing, concentrating their efforts in spreading every available canvas to catch the precious rainwater to cool their burning bodies and assuage their torturing thirst.

By 6 p.m. the storm had passed and a warm evening sun scattered the last lingering black clouds. The Austrians were still streaming, a bedraggled white torrent, across the Mincio bridges. But still no orders to try to cut off, or even harass, those still left on the west bank came from the French Emperor's headquarters. A few desultory salvoes were fired by

* Volta, his last HQ west of the river; Valeggio, the first to be set up on recrossing.

French batteries round Solferino and on Cavriana Ridge, the last being aimed at a group of horsemen moving very slowly, almost defiantly towards the Valeggio bridge. This group included the Emperor Franz Josef, Field Marshal von Hess and three Englishmen, the military attaché to Vienna, Major Redfern, Captain St George Mildmay and the *Times* correspondent, Mr Cowes. By nightfall, of the 180,000 Austrians who had crossed the river on the 23rd, only Benedek's corps in the north and the remnants of Prince Alexander of Hesse's regiment, screening the central withdrawal, remained on the west bank.

Benedek was the last to leave the battlefield, and he did so with a feeling of bitter frustration. The fighting had flared again in the north when the sun reappeared. After beating off a very half-hearted attack by Mollard's and Fanti's divisions, which then fell back in a rather disordered retreat in the direction of Lake Garda, Benedek, like a skilful boxer who has survived a flurry of courageous but unskilled assaults in the earlier rounds, sensing that his jabs and counter-punches had seriously weakened his adversary, was preparing to move in for the kill. A first lightning thrust dislodged General Durando's division from its positions at Madonna della Scoperta, from where it retreated hastily to Fenile.

It was at the moment that Benedek was about to follow up with a general attack on what gave the impression of being a rapidly disintegrating enemy that he received Franz Josef's peremptory orders to abandon his positions, fall back on the Mincio to cover the retreat of Clam-Gallas's and Stadion's corps and then himself cross over to the eastern bank. Inwardly raging, but too good, too disciplined a soldier to argue, let alone turn a deaf ear, Benedek withdrew his corps, executing the movement with a precision that could have served as a textbook example on a senior staff course. It was not till past midnight that he himself set reluctant feet on the east bank, all the more bitter in the knowledge that, without any doubt, the Piedmontese would be claiming the day as a great victory for their arms.

Technically it was a victory for Victor Emmanuel since the enemy had left him master of the battlefield, but in all justice to the Austrians, when one contemplates the victory memorial to the fallen raised proudly on the site, one should remember that, though the Piedmontese fought with exemplary courage throughout the long and bloody day, they were never able to make any impression on Benedek's defences. They were in fact retreating at the moment the Austrian commander received his orders to withdraw.

9

The Triumph and the Agony

That evening of the 24th, the mood in the three camps contrasted sharply. For not one of the three armies engaged did the past twenty-four hours constitute a simple military defeat or victory. Each felt that it was only a phase of the real struggle which had ended. A phase was dead; the next already born. In spite of the battle's awesome scale and immense significance, plans, hopes, fears could not be based on its result. Outside forces were at work which, however much they might wish to do so, not one of the three could afford to ignore.

As was only natural, the Piedmontese were jubilant, even though credit had to go once more to the French. All Lombardy was free, and it seemed that the allies were now poised to liberate Venetia. Their casualties had been heavy – over five thousand, roughly one in nine, dead or severely wounded. But from scraps of information steadily flowing in, Austrian losses were proportionately far heavier. It was open to speculation, therefore, whether the Austrians would be in a fit state to take the field for many months and, in any case, they would be suffering from a damaging inferiority complex induced by unrelieved defeat in less than two months' campaigning.

Victor Emmanuel's personal satisfaction, however, did not blind him to the fact that many obstacles were still to be overcome before the dream of Italian unity was realized.

To begin with, he was under no illusions about his ally, the French Emperor. Napoleon had promised that Italy should be 'liberated from the Alps to the Adriatic', but Victor Emmanuel had himself the gift of coining a grandiloquent phrase at the opportune moment, and he placed little value on mere words.

His brief snatched conversations with the Emperor since leaving Milan confirmed the fact that Napoleon desperately wanted a short war and would seize on the first reasonable – from his point of view – excuse to conclude an armistice and hasten his army back to France. This attitude had been made doubly clear when, on the eve of the battle, Napoleon paid a hurried visit to Victor Emmanuel's HQ to read him a letter from the Empress Eugénie stating that the Prussians seemed to be massing on the Rhine and that this had been confirmed by the Russian Ambassador, Count Schuvaloff, who warned her at the same time that any French advance into Venetia would be viewed with alarm by every country in Europe. Napoleon did not, as has been suggested, drop a broad hint that he would welcome negotiations, but Victor Emmanuel's chief of staff, General della Rocca, noted in his memoirs that 'he (the King) understood as I did, that everything was over'. A message was telegraphed to Cavour which he took so seriously that he arrived, unexpectedly, at Solferino on the evening of the 25th.

By then Victor Emmanuel had developed an optimism clothing him with a safe, spiritual armour. Napoleon might, probably would, desert him, but, like Mr Micawber, he believed that something would turn up. The road still to be travelled might be beset by a thousand perils and obstacles, but now he had no doubt that the ultimate goal would be reached, even if not in his lifetime. Physically worn out but mentally fresh, it is recorded that he slept soundly.

Once the last shot had been fired, that furious energy which had sustained Napoleon throughout the day left him. He was near to collapse, both mental and physical. Zédé recalls a significant scene after the battle as he was wandering wearily over the slopes of Cavriana Ridge, looking for a sheltered spot to pass the night:

The ground was heaped with so many corpses, Croatians and Turcos (Zouaves) and men of the 45th, that in places it was almost impossible not to step on them. But while on the ground there was this melancholy spectacle, I was struck when I looked up by the beauty of the clear sky and the view; in the background the snowy peaks of the Tyrolean Alps, nearer, the clear blue water of

Lake Garda, and all around the vast plain now a shimmering green after the downpour. I was so struck by the contrast between the beauty of nature and the fury of man, that I did not see the General with whom I was suddenly face-to-face. I stepped back and saluted, and was astonished to find myself in a ring of officers keeping respectfully in the background; only then did I recognize the Emperor. He was pacing up and down, his hands behind his back, in the same attitude that one was told was typical of his uncle; but there the resemblance ended; he seemed utterly depressed, nothing of that contented, proud, bearing one would have expected from a man who had just won a great victory. Many of my friends saw him too, and they were no more comforted by his appearance than I was, in fact we all wondered whether some very bad news were not being kept quiet ...

Napoleon had set up his HQ in Cavriana, in the same building which had been taken over by Franz Josef before he had been forced out by the French and had fallen back to Volta. After the incident related by Zédé, the Emperor returned to the bare house, ate a hurried meal, composed a brief telegram for the Empress – *'Grande bataille, grande victoire'* – then suddenly slumped over the table, his head buried in his hands, remaining in this position, neither speaking nor paying any attention to any member of his staff for several hours. On the wall behind him an unknown Austrian officer – it might even have been Franz Josef himself – had scribbled in chalk *'Addio cara Italia'* – 'Goodbye dear Italy.'

During that long meditation before climbing wearily into bed, Napoleon had made up his mind that the war must end as soon as possible. Though indifferent as to his personal safety, the mounds of dead and dying littering the battlefield shocked him profoundly; such butchery must not be prolonged. Reports of reactions in western European Courts also brought alarmed disillusion for there was, apparently, little or no enthusiasm over Franco-Piedmontese victories, and Eugénie's letter, suggesting that Prussia had partially mobilized and might be concentrating as many as 200,000 men on the Rhine, indicated that, in spite of her frequent acrimonious disputes with Austria, Prussia was not prepared to watch supinely while a fellow Germanic race was humiliated. With the cream of his army south of the Alps, Paris lay dangerously open to a determined drive from the east.

Finally there was the question of his own throne. Though now accepted and addressed as '*Mon Frère*' ('Brother') even by the Czar, and despite the birth of that longed-for heir the Prince Imperial, Napoleon did not feel that his dynasty had really taken root. Unlike the Hapsburgs, able to survive disaster after disaster, even two enemy occupations of Vienna, a *parvenu* monarch, as indeed he had described himself, risked being toppled by a minor reverse. It was essential therefore to end the campaign on a note of triumph, not risking even the suggestion of a setback, and before the sickening casualty list had time to make a serious impact – a list which a pessimistic staff officer hinted might well be inscribed with twenty thousand names.

'And so I had to give the order to retreat,' Franz Josef wrote to the Empress Elizabeth. 'I rode through a dreadful storm to Valeggio, and then drove to Villafranca ... that is the sad history of a dreadful day on which great things were done, but fortune did not smile on me. I have learned and experienced much and I know what it feels like to be a beaten general.'

For the Austrian Emperor and his staff, the night of 24 June was one of unrelieved despair. There was not a single facet of the day, unless it were Benedek's brilliant defence of San Martino, from which they could extract a grain of comfort. Losses were frightening: well over the twenty thousand mark; in addition six thousand prisoners, thirty cannon and, greatest humiliation, three regimental standards remained in enemy hands. The Hapsburg rulers of the duchies, who had been counting on an Austrian victory to restore them to their tiny realms, now gave up all hope of seeing their pleasant little palaces again. The victorious Franco-Piedmontese might, at any moment, come storming across the Mincio and, with the army in so deplorable a state, there could be no possibility of another Custozza. At the same time rumours were circulating that a French fleet was cruising off Venice. Above all for the Emperor there was the bitterness of knowing that he had failed as a man, as a leader. His pride was humbled. At this dark moment Franz Josef saw Soferino as a *personal* rather than a national humiliation.

His inner torment was such that even reports of Prussian mobilization brought him further distress. His wounded ego would not allow him to envisage outside help. Where under similar conditions both Napoleon and Victor Emmanuel would have been only too pleased to welcome a powerful ally with whose support the tables could be turned, Franz Josef was mortified by the very idea of being indebted to a third person.

'I do not feel myself to blame,' he wrote in a second letter to the Empress 'not even for faulty dispositions!'

It was a pathetic protest. As supreme head of state, as supreme commander, isolated on the summit of the lofty tower of his own creation, who else could he reasonably, logically, blame?

For the men of the three armies who had fought and survived the day's slaughter, night brought little relief, even with the business of killing halted.

After the drenching they had welcomed, men shivered in the chill night air as they endeavoured, not often with much success, to light fires to dry their sodden uniforms and restore some warmth to their weary, aching limbs. They had to fend for themselves. Anticipating the mid-twentieth-century slogan 'I'm all right, Jack', the supply services made no attempt to reach the front and bring some succour to the men who had done the fighting. In comfortable billets or equally comfortable encampments, they ate and drank those precious rations it was their duty to rush forward, while on the battlefield men, maddened by thirst, were reduced to drinking the water from muddy pools fouled by human excrement, blood and urine. Many eagerly collected this revolting viscous liquid to make a semblance of coffee, though even this was rare enough, for most of the packs (downed before a charge and their owners caught up in the vortex of combat) had been stolen or pilfered. Thousands of men not wounded simply collapsed with fatigue, weakened by hunger and thirst, falling in a coma-like sleep.

Only from Zédé's memoirs does one get a flash of humour, albeit macabre, to lighten the horrors.

The Legion, acting on its unofficial motto of '*Démerdes-toi*', a slightly crude way of saying 'The Lord helps those who help themselves', always had the best rations. At 5 p.m., though right up in the line, Zédé and a friend, a Lieutenant Astoffi, had been lucky enough to scrounge some cold chicken and wine from the resourceful regimental cook:

We got down to the serious business of eating and drinking (says Zédé) and my friend Astoffi had hold of a chicken leg which he was just bringing up to his mouth, when a bullet went through his nose and ripped open his right cheek; his comic expression as he tried to go on eating and at the same time staunch the flow of blood from his nose made me burst out laughing. (But he adds:) A moment later no one felt like laughing any more as the struggle reached a climax of fury; on our flank the Turcos and the 45th were assaulting Cavriana; twice we saw them hurled back to the bottom of the slope; after the third attack they were masters of the position but at the cost of cruel losses. Colonel Laure of the Turcos was killed, and all the senior officers and seven captains had fallen; for the last assault it was Captain Davout (son of Marshal Davout), Duke of Auerstadt, who, as the most senior officer on his feet, took command; and to think he had only served four years in the rank!'

Apart from those who strove to relieve their physical misery with warmth or some form of sustenance, the battlefield was also heaped with some forty thousand unable to move. In many ways it can be said that, of this cohort, the dead were the fortunate ones. Many of the wounded would live for a few more hours, perhaps a few more days, but in agony. Had those not wounded not been so utterly at the end of their physical resources, they would never have slept through the ghastly symphony of cries for help, moans, lamentations dragged by sheer pain from the lips of the dying.

And as a gruesome finale to this dream of horror and darkness, the battlefield was invaded by human jackals from neighbouring villages who stripped and looted the dead and dying, friend and foe alike. Nothing was sacred: the contents of the packs of men who had fought and died to free them from the Austrians, the uniforms of the dead, the contents of the pockets of the dying. Boots were ripped from gangrene-rotten feet, sometimes carrying off the foot with the boot. An attempt to resist meant a knife across the throat.

'Who will ever be able to recount all the horrors of that terrible night?' wrote the Swiss Henri Dunant. He went on to paint a vivid picture of the scene as dawn broke on the 25th: 'The most shattering spectacle that the most vivid imagination could have conjured up.'

The whole of the area was strewn with the corpses of men and horses. 'It was as if they had been sown along the roads and tracks. In ditches, ravines, hedges, fields, and above all in the immediate surroundings of Solferino .... Fields were devastated, corn and maize flattened, hedges obliterated, orchards destroyed. Pools of blood were everywhere ... houses bare skeletons, heaps of rubble ... the ground was covered with debris, shattered wagons, blood soaked fragments of clothing.'

Some effort was made to collect the wounded, but medical services were shockingly inadequate, and for a badly wounded man the only hope was a quick death and relief from inhuman suffering. Many with gaping wounds already becoming gangrenous were demented with pain, imploring any passer-by to finish them off. Equally disturbing was the sight of those who, as they lay unable to move, had had arms and legs broken by the wheels of guns passing over their prostrate bodies. The new cylindrical bullets had shattered bones and produced fractures and hideous internal tears.

Improvised hospitals were little better than slaughter houses, in spite of the efforts made by some of the local inhabitants to co-operate by allowing public buildings and even their own homes to be taken over by the medical services. An army doctor recalled that there was no separation of the wounded according to nationality, that

French, Arabs, Germans, Slavs, lay side by side. The majority were incapable of any movement. Oaths, blasphemy, heart-rending cries filled the air. The tragedy was that, although they had been picked up from the battlefield, there were so few doctors that the majority found that they had been brought into shelter so as to die in slightly less discomfort, and the *ad hoc* hospitals were no more pretty a sight than the slopes of Cavriana or the alleys of

Solferino. Untended men writhed in the convulsions of tetanus. Men with their faces black with flies, flies coagulating their wounds, looked round desperately for non-existent help. Others had uniform and flesh welded into a solid putrefying pulp. Here is a soldier his face a bloody mess, his tongue lolling from a shattered jaw. Here is a wretched man half of whose face – nose, lips, chin – has been hacked away by a sabre, dumb and half blind. Another, his skull split open, is dying, his brains spilling over the flagstones ...

The sight of so much suffering still further spurred Napoleon in his determination to call a halt to the campaign.

In the aftermath of victory (says Fleury, who accompanied Napoleon on a rapid tour of the so-called hospitals on the morning of the 25th) the Emperor appeared to be shattered. 'It's terrible,' he murmured. 'These moans are more than I can bear.' He clenched his teeth. Passing by an ambulance, he wished to visit it. An odour as if from a slaughter house emerged from the outbuilding where on hastily set-up operating tables, to the accompaniment of shrieks of pain, blood-drenched surgeons hacked away at living flesh, throwing away with apparent indifference scraps of legs and arms.

The Emperor took a few tottering steps, his kepi in his hand.

Tears ran down into his moustache.

'*La gloire coûte trop cher*,' he muttered. ('Glory costs too much.')

Then, without saying another word, he staggered outside, half fainting, sweating, mounted his charger with difficulty, riding away with his eyes half closed ...

Later in the day an official proclamation was issued:

Soldiers!
The enemy hoped to surprise us and throw us back over the Chiese; but it was he who was driven back over the Mincio. For more than twelve hours you repulsed the desperate assaults of more than 150,000 men. Your Country thanks you, but weeps as I do for those who fell on the Field of Honour.
Soldiers!
So much blood spilled for the Glory of France and the well-being of her people will not have been spilled in vain.

It was the most sober, one might almost say sombre, Order of the Day ever to greet a Napoleonic victory, the *leitmotiv* grief for the fallen rather than jubilation at victory. There could have been no clearer reflection of the Emperor's mind. And as if to emphasize sorrow for those who had given their lives, the usual spate of honours and decorations, normal epilogue of success, was missing. There was no Duke of Solferino. The only promotion was that of Niel, whose corps had stood throughout the day like a lone rock washed by the fury of the Austrian tide, from General to Marshal of France.

By evening the casualty list had been completed. It was grim enough, though not as devastating as had at first been feared: a round 12,000, of whom 782 were officers.

That evening Napoleon called a meeting of senior officers during the course of which he gave a long exposé of the international situation, as he saw it so fraught with danger, ending by declaring that, from then on, he would be thinking only of France and acting independently, whatever Piedmontese reactions. Fleury, he went on, would be sent at the first opportunity as a personal envoy to the Austrian Emperor to suggest a rendezvous to discuss terms of an immediate armistice and eventual peace. There were no dissenting voices.

Far more flamboyant was Victor Emmanuel's proclamation, containing that touch of theatricality, later to be so effectively emulated by Mussolini:

Soldati!
Nelle precedente battaglie io ebbe spesso occasione di segnalare all'
'ordine del giorno' i nomi di molti di voi. Oggi, io porto all' 'ordine
del giorno' l'intero Escercito!
(In former battles I have had occasion to mention the names of many of you in the 'orders of the day'. Today, in orders, I cite the whole Army!)

The evening of the 25th was devoted to endeavours to calm the agitated Cavour, who insisted that, rather than the ultimate victory, Solferino should be considered merely a stepping-stone to the goal of driving the last Austrian soldier from Italian soil, if needs be at the point of the bayonet. He was in fact far more worried by rumours regarding Napoleon's attitude than elated by victory. Long talks with the King and General La Marmora slightly alleviated his anxiety, however, so that he felt justified in telegraphing the Turin Parliament: 'Difficulties, though serious, are not as great as reports would have us believe.'

The 26th was spent in further talks, and on the 27th Napoleon, unwillingly, one imagines, agreed to grant Cavour an interview. Though there are no official records of the conversation, there is not the slightest doubt that the Emperor deliberately misled Cavour regarding his intentions. There was no question of an immediate peace, he stressed, at the same time shifting the blame for his apparent lack of enthusiasm for continuing the campaign onto the fact that there had been, so he gathered, a very poor response to a call for recruits to swell the depleted Piedmontese army. France, he argued, could hardly be expected to continue making such immense sacrifices in men, if the Piedmontese themselves showed such a marked reticence in risking their lives for their own country and its liberation. The Prime Minister was evidently taken in by these spurious reasonings. He left Solferino the same day, reaching Turin in record time, and immediately set himself to the task of rallying his fellow-countrymen to the flag, amongst other measures sending a strongly worded despatch to Signor Vigliano, the Governor of Milan, and an envoy, Count di Salmour, to Naples, to try to conclude an offensive alliance with the King.

The 25th and 26th brought no solace for the Austrians. Franz Josef was greeted by further bad news at Verona: confirmation of his fears that the Treasury coffers were so near empty that the maintenance of so colossal an army was a quasi-impossibility; rumours that Hungary was on the verge of an uprising and that some Hungarian units, as Hess reported, were likely to desert *en masse* should hostilities break out. Brooding, despairing, still searching in his mind for a suitable scapegoat, he was more than ready to grasp at the offer of peace he was shortly to receive, as heaven-sent.

But basically one mystery remains unsolved regarding the battle of Solferino. Why, after so desperate a struggle, after such terrible losses, after living through agonizing moments when defeat, or at least stalemate, seemed to be facing him, did Napoleon not give orders for a determined pursuit when at last the enemy was seen to be reeling back, apparently having lost all stomach for the fight? Vigorously harried, the Austrian retreat must have degenerated into a *sauve qui peut*. It is doubtful if one half of those who eventually reached the east bank would have done so had the crossing of the Mincio been contested. Instead of 22,000, Austrian losses in killed, wounded and prisoners could well have topped the 100,000 mark.

Many reasons have been put forward – the storm's effect on the terrain, Napoleon's physical exhaustion much in evidence later, his horror at the slaughter, his desire not to inflict too great a humiliation on the Austrian Emperor. At the best they are flimsy. If the terrain permitted a retreat, it could not have halted an advance. In any case the deluge lasted a bare hour. By 6 p.m., the sun had reappeared. Throughout the day Napoleon had showed astonishing energy; it was not till much later that his sudden killing fatigue struck him, and it was only then, some time after the last shot had been fired, that he was able to measure the carnage and the suffering the day had entailed. It is true that the effect of casualties on home opinion always haunted him, but as he saw the Austrians falling back, some in disorder, he was not to know that Franz Josef would be willing to agree to an armistice, or that a third major battle on, as it were, Austrian home ground – the Mincio's east bank and the area of the famous Quadrilateral – would not have to be fought, whereas a determined attack while his own men were, though weary, drunk with their own success, would have smashed, definitely, the enemy's military potential, thus automatically avoiding further French casualties.

The personal aspect may have played a subconscious role. Both he and the Empress Eugénie liked and admired the Austrian Emperor. On the other hand, although the two families were allied by marriage since Clothilde of Savoy had become the wife of Prince Napoleon ('Plon-Plon'), Napoleon could never overcome an instinctive dislike of Victor Emmanuel and, even worse, a basic mistrust. He could not help feeling that, were the King to become too successful, were Piedmont to become too powerful under so ruthless and ambitious a monarch, she might well prove an uncomfortable neighbour.

But more than for any abstract, metaphysical reasons, the explanation of Napoleon's grave tactical failure most probably lies in his lack of experience as a commander of a mass of such vast porportions as two field armies, especially when this was combined with a natural leaning to over-caution. He did not fully grasp the fact that final victory was as good as won, once von Wimpffen's criminal disobedience of direct orders turned a promising offensive into a demoralizing retreat, or that he had been presented with the opportunity of making Solferino a turning-point in history by the total annihilation of the enemy on the field – not, that is, until too late, when all but Prince Alexander of Hesse's decimated regiment, acting as rearguard, had safely reached the far side of the Mincio.

One may also find something of the atavistic in this lapse.

It should not be forgotten that the great Napoleon's refusal to commit the Imperial Guard had robbed the victory of Borodino of its just fruits.

10

The Bitter Peace

During the 25th the Austrian army moved slowly from the east bank of the Mincio and retired behind the Adige, Franz Josef remaining a prey to his blackest moods, knowing that something must be done, yet unable to decide what. His whole behaviour in the hours following the battle amply justified a later remark of Napoleon's that he was a 'man of talent but sadly lacking in energy and willpower'.

After a brief halt at Villafranca to set up an advance HQ, he then returned to Verona, from where, a bare eight days previously, he had officially assumed supreme command, and where for the first time something of the crushing weight of despair began to lift. Though no amount of self-deception could conceal the brutal fact that Austrian arms had received a shattering blow, information now coming in indicated that the enemy victory had been very hardly won and that no attempt was being made to press home the advantage gained. No major allied formations had, in fact, crossed the Mincio.

For the moment he did not envisage seeking revenge on the battlefield, but the arrival of reinforcements and enemy hesitation encouraged a sudden glimmer of hope that his opponents might be contemplating a recourse to negotiations. He was not altogether surprised then when Fleury arrived in Verona on 7 July with just such a suggestion from Napoleon. Fleury, given a most cordial welcome and highly flattered by the attention shown him, wrote: 'The Austrian Emperor completely charmed me, and asked me all sorts of questions about the Emperor's (Napoleon's) health with a solicitude which pleased me enormously.' In such a congenial atmosphere, he had no difficulty in arranging for a meeting between the two monarchs to take place four days later, 11 July, at Villafranca.

Zédé's opinion that Napoleon was not the happy, carefree, jubilant victor one could have expected was certainly justified. As has been seen, by the evening of 25 June he was determined that nothing must stand in the way of a speedily negotiated peace, and with this object in mind he had not hesitated to hoodwink Cavour in the course of their talks on the 27th.

On his return to Turin, Cavour not only hastened to carry out the demands made by the French Emperor but, lulled into a false sense of security that the alliance was in no immediate danger, started on a programme of rapid meetings with British, Russian and Prussian representatives to impress on them the justice of the Piedmontese cause and its indestructibility. Inclined also to over-estimate the significance of the Austrian defeat at Solferino and willing himself to believe in Napoleon's total sincerity, he was all the more appalled on receiving a telegram from General La Marmora: 'An armistice concluded this morning at Villafranca.'

Stunned by the implications of a cease-fire at such a crucial stage, then hoping that somehow he might be able to sabotage the negotiations, he left Turin the next day with his private secretary, Count Constantino Nigra, reaching Victor Emmanuel's HQ, the Villa Melchiorre at Monzambano, in the evening of 10 July.

Over-tired, due to intense and unremitting strain, and on the verge of a nervous breakdown, Cavour had scarcely been shown into the King's presence when he burst into a torrent of reproach fringing abuse and demanded that 'something be done' to invalidate the proposed armistice. His dismay increased when Victor Emmanuel informed him not only that it was impossible to take any such steps but that the two Emperors were meeting the very next day at Villafranca to settle final terms and exchange signatures, a meeting to which he, Victor Emmanuel, had not been invited, even in the capacity of spectator. Cavour is said to have lamented loudly that Orsini had failed in his mission.

The meeting that aroused so much bitterness in the hearts of the Piedmontese duly took place, as scheduled, the following day, the 11th, in the most friendly ambience. The two Emperors greeted each other as if they were bosom and lifelong friends rather than two men who, so recently, had confronted each other on the battlefield. Franz Josef had often affected to despise the *parvenu* French monarch, but it would appear that at Villafranca he fell almost immediately under the spell of that personal charm Napoleon was able to exercise on individuals of all nations and of every stratum of society. The successful outcome was also much aided by the fact that the aim of both men was identical. Both wanted peace with the least possible delay.

Napoleon certainly had no wish to humiliate his late adversary, since he was already dreaming of an Austro-French pact to offset the Prussian menace, while Franz Josef was anxious to placate France, hoping that by so doing he might help to dissolve the Franco-Piedmontese alliance in a spirit of mutual mistrust and deception. Few conferences dealing with such momentous problems have been so brief. It was all over within an hour.

There were only five clauses:

1. The Emperors of Austria and France will favour the creation of an Italian Confederation under the Honorary Presidency of the Holy Father.
2. The Emperor of Austria cedes to the Emperor of France all his rights upon Lombardy except the fortresses of Mantua and Peschiera. The Emperor of France will hand over this territory to the King of Sardinia (*sic*). Venice will form part of the Confederation remaining in the possession of Austria.
3. The Grand Duke of Tuscany and the Duke of Modena will return to their states, proclaiming a general amnesty.
4. The two Emperors will ask the Holy Father to introduce into his states indispensable reforms.
5. A general amnesty.

Both Napoleon and Franz Josef had obtained exactly what they wanted, and the latter could count himself exceptionally lucky to be so little despoiled after so complete a defeat; his pettiness in wishing to administer a snub to Piedmont by insisting that Lombardy first be ceded – even if only on paper – to 'the

Emperor of France', is certainly not to be admired. Napoleon, for his part, though extremely relieved by the outcome of the negotiations, was under no illusions as to Victor Emmanuel's reactions on reading the terms and especially the clauses relating to the retention of the Mantua and Peschiera fortresses, and of the whole of Venetia.

The dreaded confrontation – it was one of Napoleon's most vulnerable points that he had a profound horror of a 'scene', either political or domestic – came even earlier than he had feared, for on arriving back at Valeggio's Casa Morelli, temporary French headquarters, he found Victor Emmanuel waiting to learn the worst.

The atmosphere surrounding the encounter was icy.

Napoleon tried desperately hard to translate the agreement in the most pro-Piedmontese light possible, but it was an uphill task. The practical Victor Emmanuel saw at a glance that this treaty of Villafranca was little better than a bare-faced betrayal of the cause of Italian unity. Not bothering with the formal polite exchanges demanded by protocol, he rode back to Monzambano. He had not given up, however.

In the afternoon Napoleon received a visit from General La Marmora sent to express the King's supreme dissatisfaction. All that Napoleon was prepared to suggest or concede was that, when he came to sign, Victor Emmanuel should add the phrase 'as far as it concerns me'. Unable to achieve anything more concrete, La Marmora returned disconsolate and on edge. At ten o'clock that same night, Victor Emmanuel, accompanied by an ADC, General Solaroli, and Count Nigra, was back in Valeggio, reaching the Casa Morelli at the same time as Prince Napoleon. 'Plon-Plon' had been sent to Verona to bring back the Treaty duly signed by Franz Josef in order that it could be made valid by the signatures of both Napoleon and Victor Emmanuel.

'Plon-Plon' reported that Franz Josef had lapsed back into a rather bitter mood and had remarked, 'I trust, Prince, that you will never find yourself in the position of having to sign away your most treasured possession.' The King was not interested. In silence he added his signature to the document and, after adding 'en ce qui me concerne', left the room followed by Solaroli and Nigra.

At the Villa Melchiorre, the agitated Cavour awaited them. Nigra showed him a copy he had taken of the document while Victor Emmanuel divested himself of his tunic, opened his shirt, lighted a cigar and had himself served a glass of wine.

All his forebodings confirmed at his first glance, Cavour made another appalling scene.

'The King could never ratify such a treaty,' he raged. 'It dishonoured the royal house of Savoy, betrayed Italy, ruined at one blow the whole policy of the Government. Lombardy? What was Lombardy compared to Italian independence? Let the King refuse Lombardy; abdicate; carry on the war alone; anything to show Europe the fatal consequences of such terms and uphold the honour of Italy!'

Beside himself with frustrated passion, he offered his resignation. Victor Emmanuel tried to soothe him, failed, accepted the resignation, then in turn lost his temper. 'Things always come right for you,' he said angrily, 'for you settle them by resignation. I am the one who cannot get out of a difficulty so nicely. I cannot offer my resignation. I cannot desert the cause. We work together all right until a difficulty arises, then I am left alone to face the music. I am the one who is responsible before history and the country.'

Cavour tried to protest, but Victor Emmanuel raised his hand to signify that the discussion was closed for the time being.

'You are in no condition to carry on,' he said sharply. 'Go and get some rest; sleep will help you to regain your calm and usual sound common sense. We will talk again tomorrow.'

When talks were duly resumed, Prince Napoleon was present, more as a friend – he was, after all, the King's son-in-law – than in an official capacity. He promised that he would use all his influence with the French Emperor to get him to promise not to intervene with French arms to force the return of the Hapsburgs to the duchies from which they had been chased by their subjects. He felt sure he would succeed in this mission, as he knew his cousin's one desire was to get himself and his army back to France at the earliest possible moment. Slightly mollified, Cavour returned next morning to Turin, but muttering *Tornaremo a conspirare* ('We will become conspirators again'). The next few days were spent in handing over office, since his resignation still stood, but in the certain knowledge that it would only be a matter of months before he was recalled.

Napoleon did, in fact, give his secret consent to 'Plon-Plon's proposals, and it was on this note of conciliation that the two monarchs made a second joint entry into an Italian city – this time the Piedmontese capital, Turin.

The 'Victory Parade' led by King and Emperor was staged on 15 July to the accompaniment of deafening cheers. The citizens of Turin were welcoming back their own King, conqueror, in their eyes, of the hated Austrians on the field of San Martino, as they thought of it.* But if Napoleon did look about him, he could not have failed to notice that on many balconies and windows, the picture displayed next to that of Victor Emmanuel framed not his image but that of Orsini.

The Emperor had a last talk with Cavour after a state banquet which the latter refused to attend. Again he tried hard to excuse himself for breaking his pledged word. To carry on the fight, he insisted, he would have needed an army of at least 300,000 men, and this he could not raise; an armistice was, therefore, a military necessity. Nevertheless he again promised to exercise all his influence to prevent a *forcible* return of the duchies to their former Hapsburg rulers. Finally, as this strained, unofficial conference was ending, he turned away from Cavour and, addressing Victor Emmanuel, said abruptly, 'Your Government will pay me the expenses of the war, and we will forget about Nice and Savoy.'†

Victor Emmanuel made no reply; he simply shrugged his shoulders. Nor was there a further meeting prior to Napoleon's departure the next day. Though angry and disappointed, the King was not entirely dissatisfied after again weighing up the situation in his cold, logical mind. Despite his disillusionment that the alliance on which he had set so much store should have proved so ephemeral, he still found much encouragement on reviewing the results of the six weeks war.

---

* In most Italian histories, Solferino is always known as San Martino.
† See Appendix III.

Lombardy was his without dispute. Never again would the Austrian flag fly over Milan. With the promise that no forcible restoration of the duchies would be tolerated, it was only a question of time before a few judiciously planned insurrections combined with a renewed diplomatic offensive brought them into Piedmont's fold. Looking ahead – and he was a man always prepared to wait – he had the comfortable conviction that the South, Naples and Sicily would soon follow suit. Furthermore, as far as the vital question of national honour was concerned, 1859 had wiped out the stain of 1849.

Even if it did not come in his lifetime, he confided to his new Prime Minister, the solid old soldier La Marmora, 'Solferino has assured the future of Italy.'

He was being unduly conservative in his estimate.

In just two years, in 1861, the King of Piedmont and Sardinia became Victor Emmanuel II of Italy.

He and Napoleon would never again meet face to face, though their paths were to cross politically on several occasions, not always amicably. As the years passed, Victor Emmanuel demonstrated that he possessed that trait popularly associated with elephants: a capacity to nurse a grudge for an unlimited period. If he genuinely desired to gratify an ever-present yearning for revenge's proverbial sweetness, he certainly grasped the occasion offered in France's black hours of the late summer of 1870.

Realizing that he had made a fatal error in allowing himself to be bludgeoned into war with Prussia, Napoleon made desperate attempts to enlist the aid of both Austria and the young state of Italy.

Victor Emmanuel played cat and mouse with his son-in-law 'Plon-Plon', sent as envoy, as is shown by the latter's telegrams: 'Italy will do what she can diplomatically'; 'Italy is favourably disposed, but incapable of military action for at least one month.' 'Plon-Plon' went on to say that, 'If only our army could win a success in the field, it would help enormously.' But as Napoleon said bitterly, if the French were able to beat the Prussians unaided, they would not be grovelling for foreign support. It was indeed the aftermath of Villafranca.

The last word in this beneath the surface feud was spoken by the indomitable Empress Eugénie. Napoleon himself was dead, resting in his grave at Chislehurst, and Louis, the Prince Imperial, a cadet at the Royal Military Academy, Woolwich, the 'Shop'. In the summer of 1876, Eugénie decided that she and her son should embark on a Continental tour which inevitably included a formal visit to the Italian Court. The ex-Empress had always disliked Victor Emmanuel, had been on distant terms with his daughter Clothilde and was never tired of repeating that but for Magenta and Solferino there might never have been a Piedmontese survival, let alone a new-born Italy.

When she and the Prince Imperial were shown into the King's salon, 'she noticed the walls were smothered with photographs and portraits of the Hohenzollerns, but not even a small likeness of Napoleon III was anywhere to be seen. Victor Emmanuel remarked his guest's stormy expression and asked, 'Are you astonished at what you see?' 'No!' replied Eugénie bitingly, 'I am astonished by what I do *not* see.'

Napoleon, however, could never have envisaged the tragedy of 1870 when he returned to his own capital. Paris gave him and his army a rapturous welcome. His 'victory parade' was truly the apogee of the Second Empire. The whole of France bathed in a renaissance of *'la gloire'*, extolling Magenta and Solferino as names to be inscribed in the book of fame alongside those of Austerlitz, Iena, Friedland and Wagram.

Eugénie had played her part in the creation of this moment of euphoria. As soon as Napoleon's telegram of the evening of 24 June was received, she ordered a solemn *Te Deum* to be sung at Notre Dame. Forty years later, an exile, a widow, having lost her son in a minor colonial war which, in any case, was no concern of France, she remembered the day wistfully. 'There were moments when we were so deafened by the cheering that we passed the bands without hearing the music. On our way back (from Notre Dame) we were pelted with flowers; they were like bullets beating on the breastplates of the *Cent-Gardes* ... my son was trembling with excitement, clapped his hands and threw kisses to the crowds. Then, too, I had the glorious certainty that God had designed for my child the task of crowning his father's labours.'

The day was 14 August 1859, Feast of the Assumption of the Virgin Mary and the ninetieth anniversary of the birth of the first Napoleon. In the saddle of a magnificent charger brought from Britain, Napoleon III rode at the head of his troops from the Place de la Bastille to the Place Vendôme. It was the third such 'victory parade' he had led that year, and at that moment who would have dared to prophesy that, in the century to come, those same streets and boulevards would twice ring to the tread of the boots and hoofs of a foreign army?

Yet in the midst of this outburst of national pride and joy, of such a unique demonstration of loyalty to the Empire, one doubting voice was raised, inspired one would have said by near clairvoyance. Strangely enough, it was that of General Fleury, the devoted friend and admirer. The army, he writes,

after concentrating at the Place de la Bastille, the Emperor at its head, paraded the length of the boulevard before an immense crowd, the National Guard and the Paris garrison lining the route. When the conquered Austrian standards and cannons, each escorted by a guard from a different regiment, appeared, cries of *Vive l'Empereur* rang out exultantly. Imperial France demonstrated her pride in herself and her sovereign. A prophet of evil who would have dared to predict that this triumphal scene would be the last of the Empire's few remaining years would certainly have been looked upon askance. Yet why not confess it today? In the middle of their cries of joy which inebriated the senses of even the wisest, I felt a tightening of the heart. I kept telling myself that the Emperor had done wisely in making peace, yet the thought kept nagging me – diminishing the merit of this act of moderation – that an unfinished victory can only bring trouble in its wake.

Franz Josef's bitter mood was again upon him when he signed the Villafranca Treaty, as evidenced by his remark to Prince Napoleon. The observation was a measure of the pain the loss of Lombardy was causing him and which, he knew, would be reflected in Vienna, where public opinion was still stunned by the flood of bulletins recounting disasters piling up with such rapidity, and as the magnitude of the calamity became apparent, numbness was turning to anger.

It did not seem possible that any monarch, especially an

absolute monarch, could survive the results of such bungling and ineptitude.

At the beginning of the year 1859, Austria was in a dominant position both politically and, on paper at any rate, militarily. That she had now fallen so low was her Emperor's fault since in a state of absolutism, subordinates cannot legitimately be expected to take a share of blame. Furthermore, the idiotic ultimatum which had provoked the war revealed his political folly and immaturity, Solferino his basic inability to conduct a battle. In his personal dealings with his peers he had mortally offended the Prussian monarch, and within his own boundaries he had failed to calm Hungarian aspirations. On the eve of leaving Verona for Vienna, he received a visit from one of his cabinet ministers who not only warned that Hungarian revolt was imminent but also told him bluntly that discontent in the capital had reached such a pitch that people were saying openly that the Emperor should abdicate in favour of his younger brother, the popular Archduke Maximilian.

But what he lacked in talent, Franz Josef made up for in pure obstinacy and the courage often born of obstinacy. Not for one second, he told the cabinet minister, would he even consider abdication. Having mounted the throne, only death could remove him from it. The will of the people meant nothing to him. Though he did entertain a genuine paternal affection for his subjects, he thought of them as ignorant children to be guided in all matters by his fatherly hand. That the children might in fact be adults with wills of their own, never occurred to him.

In what seems something of a contradiction to the principle of absolutism, Franz Josef now made up his mind that there must be scapegoats to appease public wrath. Buol and Gyulai had already been dismissed. Now it was the turn of Grunne and Hess. Grunne was simply demoted to the innocuous post of Master of the Horse, but the old Field Marshal who had served his country so well was pushed into the oblivion of total retirement and made to understnad that, without making any attempt to justify himself, he must bear the official blame for every error, tactical and strategical, to which could be ascribed the defeat. It was a strange form of moral blackmail, the ultimate test of loyalty, which Franz Josef was to apply again to Count Benedek after the even greater disaster of Sadowa.*

There were enquiries into commissariat scandals responsible for the fact that on the morning of 24th June men had gone hungry and thirsty into battle. General Eynatten, the Quartermaster General, was arrested and committed suicide in his cell. Yet even in this most justifiable of probes into corruption, Franz Josef made another terrible mistake. He allowed poison tongues to undermine his relations with one of his oldest, most trustworthy, most loyal servants, his Minister of Finance, von Bruck, of whom it was said, 'He had done more to keep the Empire a going concern since 1848 than any other individual with the exception of Felix Schwarzenberg.' In a personal letter he intimated to von Bruck that he would be 'allowed' to retire. The letter reached the Finance Minister on his return home from a performance at the opera. Bruck was so heartbroken at the realization that he was no longer trusted that he promptly slashed his throat with a razor.

Franz Josef had learnt 'one more lesson the hard way ... besides knowing what it felt like to be a defeated general, he also knew what it felt like to be responsible for the death of a faithful servant ...'.

One good, however, eventually emerged from the slaughter of 24 June.

'Would it not be possible to create societies in every European country whose aim would be to assure that prompt and devoted care is given to those wounded in battle?'

The words were written by the Swiss Henry Dunant in his book *Un Souvenir de Solferino*, published a few months after the campaign and which was soon to be translated into every major European tongue. As has been seen, Dunant was appalled by the savagery of the actual fighting, but even more by the unbelievable suffering of the wounded, the lack of medical services in all three armies, the primitive treatment dispensed by the few doctors present, and the shocking inadequacy of the so-called nursing, resulting in a horrifying percentage of death from wounds which should never have proved fatal.

He was particularly distressed by the fate of the Austrian

* See Appendix II.

wounded. Since they had been abandoned by their retreating companions, they were left to the not always very tender mercies of the victors.

A spirit of neo-chivalry still existed to a certain degree amongst the officers. Dunant, himself noted that 'many Austrian officers were allowed to keep their swords. They were given exactly the same food as the French officers, and those wounded were taken care of by the same doctors.' Matters were very different where the 'other ranks' were concerned. The sound of limb, together with the walking wounded, 'were herded together like cattle and sent marching down the road to Brescia'. Dunant also had the horrible suspicion that, when mass graves were dug to get rid of the putrefying corpses whose foul odour was poisoning the air, 'in the hurry to get the unpleasant job done as quickly as possible, more than one living man was buried with the dead'. Many were certainly left to perish where they lay, priority for what little medical attention was available being given to allied troops. 'Many of the young soldiers from the diverse provinces of the immense Hapsburg Empire had just dropped in their tracks from sheer fatigue and inanition; weakened by loss of blood, even though only slightly wounded, they died miserably of exhaustion and hunger; without care, without succour.'

But of all the nightmarish scenes, it was that of the many amputations which most affected the young Swiss, when patients were subjected to a torture which could scarcely have been surpassed in any medieval dungeon. With a fascinated horror he describes how

the surgeon had removed his jacket, rolling up his sleeves, and donning a large apron. Then with one knee on the flagstones of the bare room, he encircled the soldier's thigh with his left arm, holding a terrible-looking knife in his right hand. With one blow he slashed open the skin above the wound. A piercing scream echoed round the hospital.

'Courage' said the doctor to the soldier in a low voice. 'Another couple of minutes and it will all be over.'

He began to pull the flesh back until the muscles were exposed, then, with another blow, severed all the muscles to the bone. A torrent of blood spurted from the arteries, smothering the surgeon himself and splashing like a fountain on the floor.

'Oh. Oh!' moaned the tortured man. 'It's too much. Please let me die.'

'Just one more minute,' said the surgeon's assistant. It was the moment to use the saw, and within seconds one heard its metallic grinding as it bit into the exposed, half gangrenous bone.

But the pain was too much for this weakened, worn-out body; the groan died away, he had fainted. No longer guided in his work by the patient's screams, the surgeon looked at him anxiously, fearing that he was dead. The extra strong drink kept in reserve for extreme cases only just managed to bring back a little animation to his expressionless eyes. He might or might not live, but at least his suffering was over ...

As what might serve as a slow curtain to this drama, Dunant added that another forty thousand who died or were permanently incapacitated by minor wounds which never healed or by lingering maladies attributable to the hardships of the days immediately preceding or following the battle, had to be added to the forty thousand killed or severely wounded on the 24th. In fact, 'if one can forget the glamour and glory of military achievement, this Solferino battle must be counted a disaster from the point of view of humanity!'

Dunant's best-seller, as well as evoking such hideous images, achieved a concrete and lasting result. From 26 to 29 October inclusive, a European conference was convened at Geneva, its object 'to study the means of overcoming the insufficiency of the sanitary services in campaigning armies'.

The conference was fully attended, the spirit of eager co-operation shown by all representatives was remarkable, and from it emerged the original Geneva Convention, comprising ten articles 'for the betterment of wounded soldiers in time of war'. The completed document was drawn up, ready for signature, on 'the twenty second day of the month of August of the year one thousand eight hundred and sixty four'.

Epilogue

There could be no doubt as to who had emerged victorious from the brief campaign which ended on the bloody field of Solferino, but for Piedmont the victory savoured somewhat of an unfinished symphony. Victor Emmanuel might call himself King of Italy – by the grace of His Majesty the Emperor Napoleon III of France – but, regarded dispassionately, it was, under the circumstances, a near derisory title. Victor Emmanuel and Cavour were fully aware of this, as was the other great patriot, Garibaldi. All three were determined not to accept Villafranca as the final word but to carry on to bring the struggle to its veritable conclusion. For them the fundamental aim could be summed up in the words of the poet Luigi Mercantini, who, at the beginning of the campaign, had composed the song '*Va fuori d'Italia, va fuori, o stranier!*' – 'Out of Italy, get out, foreigner!'

They were encouraged in their hopes by the fact that the war had been the signal for unrest and minor uprisings in the duchies of Parma and Modena, in the Romagna and in the Marches. The Italian people were again making it clear that their only desire was to be integrated into a state of Italy that would embrace the whole of the peninsula under the crown of Piedmont.

Europe, however, had still to be cured of the belief that the powers qualified as 'major' had earned an almost hereditary right to interfere in the domestic affairs, the government or governments, that should rule the country. Napoleon was broadcasting the fact that he was dedicated to the idea of a federation. Austria was far from reconciled to the fact that her influence had come to an end. Britain, Prussia and Russia all obstinately demanded their say in the future. The bitter disappointment of Italians after the terms of Villafranca were made public can well be understood. Many, probably, echoed Cavour's furious outburst: 'The Emperor (Napoleon) has dishonoured me!'

By the time the terms of what might be called the 'phoney' treaty were signed, the duchies of Parma and Modena had ousted their Austrian rulers and been amalgamated into a single state under the dictatorship of a close friend of Cavour's, a one-time editor of *Il Risorgimento*, Luigi Carlo Farini. Farini then proceeded to take over the Romagna, which, with the two duchies, he declared would be a single state under the name of Emilia, till formal annexation by Piedmont. During this same period another friend of Cavour's, Baron Bettino Ricasoli, made himself ruler of Tuscany, also making it clear that his rule was to be purely temporary till Tuscany, in turn, became an integral part of the kingdom of Piedmont/Italy.

On 10 August Ricasoli concluded a pact with Farini whereby an army of forty thousand raised, jointly by Emilia and Tuscany, came under the command of General Fanti.

Austria's reply was to threaten to boycott yet another conference that had opened in Zurich to work out a 'final' and, hopefully, binding peace. Surprisingly, there was opposition also from Napoleon on hearing of the moves inaugurated by Ricasoli and Farini, who made the astonishing statement that through all his life he had been, and still remained, a firm supporter of Italian independence, he did *not* consider Italian unity desirable because 'unity would involve me in internal perils by reason of Rome, and France would not be pleased to see the rise on her flank of a great nation that might be capable of diminishing her influence.'

10 November saw the signing of the Zurich treaty. It was a very anaemic document which gave no satisfaction to either of the principal parties concerned. No action was suggested for the restoration of the disgruntled rulers who had been forced to flee their duchies and provinces. But at the same time there was no positive mention of a kingdom of a united Italy. Victor Emmanuel was bitterly disappointed, and the rebuff, as he saw

it, may have prompted him, though still angry with Cavour, to re-form the team which had pursued Piedmont's struggle with such success in the early days and throughout the war. Cavour was recalled to Turin to combine the offices of President of the Council and Minister of Foreign and of Home Affairs.

His first move was to try to restore good relations with France. A personal letter to Napoleon contained the suggestion that he support the idea of a plebiscite of the population of central Italy in return for the cession of Savoy, and eventually Nice, despite Garibaldi's opposition. The offer was then formalized in the office of the Foreign Ministry on 24 March 1860.

The plebiscite in central Italy went ahead with Napoleon's blessing. The question to which the individual was requested to reply 'yes' or 'no' was: 'Union to the constitutional monarchy of Victor Emmanuel or a separate kingdom?' The young state of Emilia voted overwhelmingly for union, 426,000 against 765, while Tuscany returned 366,571 'yes' and 14,935 'no'. Even the Pope's decree excommunicating those who had connived at the secession of the Romagna from the Papal States could not mar the outburst of joy greeting the results, and the moment when the newly formed state, together with Tuscany became, formally the kingdom of Northern Italy on 2 April.

While the Powers continued their apparently unending arguments, Garibaldi felt that the time for definite action had arrived. The general mood of caution in Turin both exasperated and frustrated him. With the outbreak of further riots in the south provoked by the results of the plebiscites, he saw a chance of destroying the foreign kingdom of Naples by a single bold, though extremely risky, stroke.

The most serious incidents had occurred in the Sicilian capital of Palermo in April. Though the revolt had been speedily and brutally repressed by the Austrian garrison, the leaders duly executed, trouble continued sporadically all over the island. But while Garibaldi was mustering an invasion force in Genoa, news came through that the last centre of resistance had been wiped out. Nevertheless, having recruited some twelve thousand men, he embarked with his volunteers at Quarto, in the vicinity of Genoa, on 6 May on two steamships, the

Piemonte and the *Lombardo*, appearing off Talamona, after having picked up a contingent of Tuscans, the following day.

As a deception move, Garibaldi landed a force the equivalent of a strong battalion to thrust into Papal States territory. However, when confronted by papal forces, the little column promptly retreated, as planned, to fall back across the border of what, till recently, had been the province of Tuscany.

While these skirmishes took place, successfully diverting attention, the main body sailed on, reaching Sicily in the vicinity of Marsala on 11 May and disembarking without loss despite the attempted intervention of two Neapolitan cruisers.

By first light on 12 May, Garibaldi, at the head of his expeditionary force which would go down in history as 'The Thousand', marched inland to reach the town of Salemi. There, from the market square, he proclaimed that he had annexed Sicily in the name of King Victor Emmanuel and that he had appointed himself temporary governor of the island in the King's name. Three days later, on the 15th, his vanguard ran into a strong Neapolitan defensive position covering the town of Calatafimi. The Neapolitans resisted so strongly that Garibaldi was advised to break off the action. His reply was typical: 'Here we make Italy or die.'

The attacks were renewed with such vigour that the Thousand stormed a dominating hilltop, whereupon the remainder of the Neapolitan force abandoned its positions to fall back in some disorder on Palermo. The ensuing battle for the Sicilian capital lasted ten days. But on 7 June the bulk of the garrison was tricked into making a sortie which led them straight into a cleverly prepared ambush, after which the Garibaldians forced their way into the city at the point of the bayonet. On 8 June there were pleas for an armistice, and the Sicilian capital passed into Garibaldi's hands. The disgruntled Neapolitans attempted one last stand at Milazzo. There was a brief lull in operations allowing the Thousand to receive reinforcements from Piedmont. Then, on 20 July, Garibaldi renewed his offensive on Milazzo, destroying the remnants of the enemy army.

These victories now began to cause Victor Emmanuel some embarrassment.

Generally speaking, Europe was apprehensive of Garibaldi's success, haunted always by the fear of 'revolution' which he seemed to embody. To appease Napoleon, a message was sent to Garibaldi forbidding him to cross the Straits of Messina and pursue his campaign on the mainland. Garibaldi, however, considered he was in a position to ignore the order. On 19 August the Straits were crossed to begin an advance on Naples, the Thousand everywhere acclaimed as 'liberators' by the local population.

The Neapolitan king, Francis II, fled the city precipitately on 6 September, allowing the 'liberators' to make their entry unopposed the next morning, wildly cheered by the inhabitants thronging the streets.

This unexpectedly easy success inspired the Turin government to take what was to prove a decisive step forward to the final achievement of its goal. Turin suddenly informed the Pope that, if he did not disband the mercenary forces controlling the Papal States, who, it was alleged, were the very prototype of tradition's 'brutal and licentious soldiery', the King would be compelled to order his army to intervene. And to demonstrate that this was no idle verbal warning, a force led by General Fanti marched into papal territory.

Some days later, on the 18th, a detachment led by General Cialdini routed a contingent of the papal Gendarmerie at Castelfidardo. Profoundly discouraged and though led by one of France's most distinguished soldiers, General Lamoricière, the papal forces surrendered.

Meanwhile, to the south, a major battle was fought on 2 and 3 October, on the banks of the Volturno river. The ranks of the Thousand had been swelled to some 24,000 by local recruits flocking to serve under the tricolor, but were still heavily outnumbered by the Neapolitans who had assembled an army of at least 50,000. Nevertheless, Garibaldi won a remarkable victory ending with the complete rout of his opponents. A month later, in the first week of November, a plebiscite held on the same lines as those in central Italy resulted in 302,064, as against 10,312, voting for union with Victor Emmanuel, who did Garibaldi the honour of riding south to 'greet the conqueror'.

The meeting took place at Teano near Caserta where, according to Count Orsi, 'The popular idol saluted Victor Emmanuel as King of Italy and then in the true manner of the epic hero, withdrew to Caprara, leaving the King to complete the work he had so gloriously begun.'

Francis II was still unwilling to leave what was by now no more than a phantom kingdom. As a token of resistance he shut himself up in Gaeta. The city withstood a half-hearted siege till February 1861, but on the 12th, on coming to the inevitable conclusion that his cause was lost, he embarked on a French vessel, eventually making his way to Rome, where he lived till 1870.

On 18 February the first genuine Italian Parliament assembled in Turin. It consisted of 443 deputies and represented over 22 million people. Officially Victor Emmanuel was still the King of Piedmont/Sardinia, but this anomaly was finally corrected when, on 17 March, he signed a decree announcing that:

VICTOR EMMANUEL II
by the Grace of God
King of Sardinia, of Cyprus, and of Jerusalem
Duke of Savoy and of Genoa
Prince of Piedmont, etc., etc.
We sanction and promulgate the following –

Article one: Victor Emmanuel II, assumes for himself and his successors the title of King of Italy.

The first to give their official blessing to this new kingdom were Britain, the United States of America and Switzerland. The most bitterly opposed were Austria and the Pope.

Even now the great task was not completed. Rome and Venice still had to be gathered into the fold.

Cavour became convinced that the best hope of annexing Venice lay in the formation of an alliance with the ever-increasing power of Prussia, clearly set on a collision course with Austria in the not too distant future. As regards Rome, historically Italy's true capital, it was still a question of patience and caution, especially while Austria remained a major power, and France, largely due to the influence of the

Empress Eugénie, was being swept by a wave of clericalism. Furthermore, Rome enjoyed the protection of the French army, and as if to stress this fact, Napoleon had seen fit to send Victor Emmanuel an unambiguously frank note to the effect that any attempt by Garibaldi, who was known to favour armed confrontation, to invade the papal possessions, would be looked upon as an act of war.

It was while these two problems still awaited their solution that Cavour died of a virulent fever. Sadly his last appearance in Parliament had been marred by a furious quarrel with Garibaldi over the cession of Nice. There was, however, a reconciliation. Just under a month before his death, the ailing Cavour received a brief note from Garibaldi stating, 'Let Victor Emmanuel be the arm of Italy and you the brain. Trusting in your superior capacity and firm desire to promote the welfare of the country, I shall await that welcome voice that will call me once again to the field of battle.'

Cavour had always lacked physical charisma, but he was gifted with an incredibly lucid brain, the capability of assembling facts and from them deducing the logical solution to any problem. With Victor Emmanuel, he had formed a perfect team to accomplish one of the most remarkable political achievements of the nineteenth century.

After such a lengthy period of strife, a brief spell of outward peace settled on Europe, but towards the end of 1863 the Italian question seemed again to be simmering as rumours began to circulate that Mazzini, still in exile in London, was plotting further violence.

The following year, 1864, Garibaldi paid a visit to London, with Victor Emmanuel's approval, to confer with Mazzini. From the social point of view the visit was an immense success – the leader of the already legendary Thousand was a popular hero – but a political failure. The British Government, suspecting the real reason for Garibaldi's visit rather than the one semi-officially put forward, namely a visit to an eminent physician for treatment of a tiresome leg wound, let it be known that London had no wish to become the centre of any form of international 'revolutionary' intrigue. Most anxious not to offend so powerful a sympathizer, Victor Emmanuel promptly recalled the 'hero'.

Further requests were then addressed to Napoleon to withdraw French troops from Rome. The Emperor was prepared to consider the move but suggested that Italy should, in return, make a gesture to reassure the world that she herself had no designs on Rome by moving the seat of government from Turin to Florence. Purely to gain time, Victor Emmanuel agreed. On 15 September 1864 Florence became Italy's new capital.

Eighteen months later, in April 1866, an aggressive alliance between Prussia and Italy, aimed at Austria, was signed.

Italian armed forces had been increased to number nearly a quarter of a million men. Unfortunately there was no analogous increase in overall military efficiency. General La Marmora was then Prime Minister, and one would have imagined that under his guidance the standard of the army as an instrument of war would have been considerably enhanced. This was far from being the case. Bismarck had approached him with a view to working out a joint strategy, suggesting at the same time that Garibaldi should be given the task of harassing Austria by stirring up insurrection in Hungary and Dalmatia. La Marmora would not agree to either proposal. He detested Garibaldi and, rather than co-ordinating operations, it was his intention to limit Italy's efforts to the seizure of Venetia and the Trentino area.

Another reason for the dismal failure of Italy's role in the campaign was Victor Emmanuel's insistence on retaining supreme command. One remembers that he had greatly distinguished himself in the 1848 and '49 wars, in which he had never led a force larger than a division, and in 1859, though never lacking in personal courage, he had been completely outmanoeuvred by Benedek.

What had been shown to be Piedmont's fatal weakness at the time of Solferino was repeated in 1866: total lack of staff work and even less sense of co-operation at the higher echelons of command, the generals obsessed by petty jealousies and spite. Though nominally Commander-in-Chief, Victor Emmanuel split his force into three virtually independent commands under Generals La Marmora, temporarily renouncing his office as Prime Minister, Cialdini, and Garibaldi operating out on a limb in the Trentino area.

As in 1859, no real effort was made to manoeuvre the army as a whole, so that, when La Marmora crossed the Mincio to fight the second battle of Custozza, he found himself completely on his own with a bare third of the total force that could have been available. Battle was joined on 24 June. Again the Italians displayed great courage, but the day ended in a second defeat, it being later reported that 'the several (Italian) bodies fought without unity of control, so that the fight was not so much a set battle with a definite objective, as a series of disconnected engagements, in which the different units, having lost their bearings and lacking initiative, could do no more than give proof of individual valour. By evening the Italian army was beaten at all points and was obliged to recross the Mincio.'

The defeat was a rude shock. The King and his people now pinned their hopes on a naval victory by the fleet led by Admiral Persano to regain lost prestige. But again the almost pathological inability to establish a compact command was to prove fatal when the Austrian fleet under Admiral Tegethoff was encountered off Lissa on 20 July. 'Each of the Italian vessels fought on its own account; in fact part of the fleet remained almost inert and confined itself to useless firing from a great distance.'

Yet the Italians enjoyed numerical superiority; twenty-eight ships with 641 guns as against twenty-six ships with 532 guns. Nevertheless, thanks to superior training and discipline, the Austrians were able to concentrate the fire of their combined fleet on individual Italian ships, in some cases following up their devastating salvoes by ramming so that 'when the Italian flagship was breached and sent straight to the bottom, the rest of the fleet made off as best it could'.

By the time the Italians had regrouped and resumed the offensive, their advance being practically unopposed since the Austrians had rushed every available man north to meet the Prussian threat, the Prussians had won the crushing victory of Sadowa, or Königgratz, forcing the Austrians to sue for an armistice, at which point Napoleon had stepped in with an offer to act as negotiator.

Garibaldi, who had won the only Italian victories in the Trentino, commented bitterly on Lissa in a letter addressed to Baron Ricasoli: 'Italy possesses sailors in no way inferior to those of England and America. And again with magnificent army material, we have nevertheless fought on land hardly any better than at sea.' Showing remarkable clarity he went on: 'This is obviously due to the same defect in leadership. The worst of it is that nothing is being done to change the leadership. The men who led the way to the catastrophe of Custozza and Lissa are still at the head of affairs. And what guarantee is there that Italy will see herself restored to her dignity as a nation?'

By the Treaty of Prague, concluded on 24 August, Austria ceded Venetia to France – a repeat of the insulting terms of Villafranca – before the province was duly handed over to Italy after a plebiscite had recorded 647,246 votes, against a mere 69, in favour of unification.

Now only the question of Rome remained to be solved.

Napoleon withdrew his troops in the autumn, but Victor Emmanuel still did not feel strong enough to act unilaterally and face the storm that would inevitably follow. He even felt obliged to place Garibaldi under temporary house arrest in Caprera when he learned of a plan to recruit another Thousand and occupy the Eternal City by force of arms. Even so, a company of seventy men, raised and led by two brothers, Enrico and Giovanni Cairoli, decided to act on their own initiative. Their attempt ended in disaster. Their puny band advanced to within a couple of miles of Rome but was then confronted and completely wiped out by a vastly numerically superior papal contingent.

Matters then remained in abeyance till the outbreak of the Franco-Prussian war in 1870.

There is no doubt that Napoleon considered that he was entitled to Italian support after his massive intervention on Piedmont's side in the 1859 campaign. Victor Emmanuel, however, was above all a pragmatist. Had the two men been bound by ties of genuine personal friendship, there might have been some move, some gesture on Victor Emmanuel's part. But ever since Clothilde's marriage, after Villafranca and after the Treaty of Prague, he had felt both dislike and a nagging distrust for France's ruler. Under the circumstances, cynically, it must be admitted, he preferred to watch and wait and then profit by his former ally's humiliation.

On 11 September, by which time the French army had been virtually annihilated at Sedan, General Raphael Cadorna was ordered to lead a march on Rome. The Italian force reached the city on the 18th and there halted for two days while negotiations were being held. When these broke down, the Italians went over to the attack, breaching the walls in the vicinity of the Porta Pia. The papal troops promptly surrendered on the orders of Pope Pius IX, who then shut himself up in the Vatican. There could be no doubt as to the sentiments of the Romans. Cadorna's men were welcomed by wildly cheering crowds.

On 5 December Victor Emmanuel spoke in Florence for the last time.

'With Rome as the capital of Italy,' he declared, 'I have fulfilled my promises and crowned the undertaking which twenty-three years ago was begun by my magnanimous father. As a King and as a son, I feel in my heart a solemn joy when I greet the representatives of our beloved country assembled here, and when I pronounce these words: "Italy is free and one; it only remains for us now to make her great and happy." '

Appendix I
Order of Battle of the Three Contending Armies, 24 June

A. *The Piedmontese Army*

Commander-in-Chief	King Victor Emmanuel
Personal adviser to the C-in-C	General of the Army, La Marmora
Chief-of-Staff	General della Rocca
1st Division	General Giovanni Durando
2nd Division	General Manfredo Fanti
3rd Division	General Filiberto Mollard
4th Division	General Enrico Cialdini
5th Division	General Domenico Cucchiari
Cavalry	General Calvisto Bertone di Cambuy

B. *The French Army*

Commander-in-Chief	Emperor Napoleon III
Chief of Staff	Marshal Vaillant
1st Corps	Marshal Baraguey d'Hilliers
Divisional commanders	General Forey
	General de Ladmirault
	General Bazaine
Corps cavalry	General Devaux
2nd Corps	Marshal MacMahon, Duke of Magenta
Divisional commanders	General de la Motterouge
	General Decaen

Corps cavalry	General Gaudain de Villaine
3rd Corps	Marshal Canrobert
Divisional commanders	General Renault
	General Trochu
	General Bourbaki
Corps cavalry	General Partonneaux
4th Corps	General Niel
Divisional commanders	General de Luzy de Pelissac
	General Vinoy
	General de Failly
Corps cavalry	General Richpance
Imperial Guard	Marshal Regnault de St-Jean d'Angely
Divisional commanders	General Mellinet
	General Camou
Guards cavalry	General Morris

C. *The Austrian Army*

Commander-in-Chief	Emperor Franz Josef
Chief of Staff	Field Marshal von Hess
1st Army	*Feldzeugmeister* von Wimpffen
3rd Corps	Prince Edward von Schwarzenberg
Divisional commanders	General Schonberger
	General Habermann
9th Corps	Field Marshal Count von Schaffgotsche
Divisional commanders	General Haendel
	General Count de Crenneville
11th Corps	Field Marshal Baron von Weigel(Veigl)
Divisional commanders	General Schwarzel
	General von Blomberg

Army cavalry division	General Count Zedwitz

2nd Army	Field Marshal Count Schlick

8th Corps	Field Marshal Count von Benedek
Divisional commanders	General Berger
	General Lang

5th Corps	Count von Stadion
Divisional commanders	General Palffy
	General Sternberg

1st Corps	Count Clam-Gallas
Divisional commanders	General Count Montenuovo
	General Stankowicz

7th Corps	Baron von Zobel
Divisional commanders	General the Prince of Assia
	General Bradstein

Army cavalry division	General Baron von Mensdorff

Appendix II
Count von Benedek and Franz Josef

The Emperor's treatment of his best general presents one of the darker sides of his character: a fanatical ruthlessness that took hold of him in his dealings with any one of his subjects whenever his personal prestige seemed threatened. It became manifest in his behaviour immediately following on Solferino. Seven years later, it was the one commander who had saved Austrian military honour at Solferino who fell victim to this contemptible trait.

When war with Prussia broke out in 1866, Victor Emmanuel, seeing a golden opportunity to profit by Austria's difficulties and seize Venetia, also declared war. This meant that Austria was obliged to mobilize two armies, one to meet the Prussians in the north striking through Bohemia, the other to march southwards against the Italians. Pleading his knowledge of the country and experience in fighting the Italians, Benedek requested that he be entrusted with the southern theatre of operations. For some reason that has never been explained, Franz Josef not only refused, insisting that Benedek take over command in the north, but then deliberately intervened in the battle plan, giving Benedek formal orders to abandon his carefully worked out manoeuvre to lure the Prussians into a trap and, instead, to advance to meet the numerically superior and better-armed Prussians in an encounter battle. The result was the disaster of Sadowa (Königgratz). Once news of the defeat reached Vienna, Franz Josef hastened to place the blame squarely on Benedek's shoulders, ordering him to appear before a court martial.

As if this were not enough, he exacted a promise from the

unfortunate Field Marshal that he would make no effort to defend himself before his accusers or endeavour, in any way, to refute the charges. The most loyal of men, Benedek gave this fatal promise knowing that by so doing he was ruining himself, as was soon evident when the official government newspaper, the *Wiener Zeitung*, published a bitter attack on him, stressing that Austria's misfortunes were due entirely to the northern commander's 'criminal' errors.

Ignominiously dismissed the service, Benedek lived on for another fifteen years. After a judicious lapse of time, the Emperor could, and should, have reinstated him, but he did no such thing, fearing that such an act of justice might be translated as weakness or even an admission of guilt.

Appendix III
Nice and Savoy

It was not long before Napoleon was regretting his offer to shelve the annexation of Nice and Savoy in return for the cost of the campaign, and had reopened the question with Turin. Though initially both a little surprised and indignant, by the end of the year (1859) Victor Emmanuel was thinking that it might after all be better to part with a peripheral stretch of territory, the majority of whose inhabitants were francophone and at heart felt themselves to be more French than Italian, than to be obliged to pay out the, for those days, colossal sum of the equivalent of £30 million.

The King was well aware that the cession of any portion of Piedmontese territory would evoke furious opposition from the ultra-nationalists, and especially from Garibaldi, himself a native of Nice, but he reckoned that by shrewd bargaining tremendous overall advantages could be gained, in particular if a promise from Napoleon could be extracted that he should turn a blind eye to the incorporation of Tuscany and the Romagna into the kingdom of Piedmont after the formality of a plebiscite, the result of which was a foregone conclusion.

Napoleon was willing to fall in with these plans, but surprisingly, when news leaked of this purely private agreement, it raised a storm in Britain. Napoleon was not popular in the British Isles. Despite the indisputable success of the mutual visits the reigning families had paid each other, Britain was always ready to look upon France, especially a Napoleonic France, as a potential menace and to credit the Emperor's least action with sinister intent. This unjustifiable political phobia was well summed up by Lord Palmerston: 'I had strong confidence in the frank intentions of Napoleon towards England, but of late I have begun to feel great distrust and to suspect that his formerly announced intention of avenging Waterloo has only lain dormant and has not died away.'

France and Piedmont were certainly taken aback by Britain's aggressive attitude over what was, after all, a personal matter between the two monarchs, and considering that a mere glance at the map was enough to make clear how very small was the area involved – an area, moreover, which geographically and linguistically was a natural apanage of France. Cavour who, as expected, returned to power in January 1860, found himself very much on the horns of a dilemma when, in spite of Napoleon's assurance, 'Since Villafranca I have only had one thought and one aim – to inaugurate a new era of peace and to live on good terms with all my neighbours, especially England' – the Piedmontese Government was informed that, 'In the opinion of Her Majesty's Government, the King of Sardinia (sic) will besmirch the arms of the House of Savoy if he yields to France the cradle of his illustrious and ancient House.'

After discussing the matter at great length and from every angle, Victor Emmanuel and Cavour decided in the end that material considerations must prevail. Though the King had not really forgiven Cavour for his post-Solferino resignation, he was never a man to cut off his nose to spite his face and, respecting his Prime Minister's political acumen, was prepared to listen carefully to his arguments.

Both saw that the one real danger to a united Italy, even to the very existence of the kingdom of Piedmont and Sardinia, remained Austria. Franz Josef's huge, though unwieldy, Empire possessed an almost inexhaustible source of manpower. He could lose an army of 150,000 men only to replace it in a very brief space of time with another of the same size, or even greater. Because of this permanent threat, the friendship of both Britain and France was highly desirable. Piedmont, therefore, was placed in a most invidious situation when it became apparent that whatever action she took 'must offend the one or the other, for the cession of Savoy, while it would placate France would anger England, while its refusal, which would please England, would alienate Napoleon'.

It was the choice of the lesser of two evils, and eventually both men agreed on the way this choice must be orientated so as to minimize the Austrian menace.

Though Britain was admired and respected, neither the King nor Cavour believed she would be prepared to send an expeditionary force to stand and fight side by side with the Piedmontese should Austria, motivated by a spirit of revenge, launch an invasion to recover her lost provinces. France on the other hand could, and possibly would. Having come to this painful decision, an envoy, Count Arese, was sent to Paris immediately, to discuss final details in the face of both British and Austrian opposition.

Excessively tough bargaining followed, especially when Piedmont insisted that the cession of Savoy must be compensated by the annexation of Tuscany with total French backing. Tempers became frayed, flared. There were even moments when it looked as if diplomatic relations between the two countries were on the point of being broken off, particularly towards the end of February when Cavour wrote to Count Arese ordering him not to yield one iota in his demands. 'I shall be desolated to be abandoned by the Emperor,' ran the letter, 'but, I repeat it, I believe it better to run the risk of being crushed by Austria than to lose all prestige and to be reduced to govern only by bayonets. For nations as for individuals, there are circumstances when the voice of honour speaks louder than that of prudence.'

Napoleon finally gave way, suggesting that the enlargement of the kingdom of Piedmont by the inclusion of Tuscany necessitated 'as a safety measure for France a demand for the French slopes of the mountains', in other words Savoy. 24 March, 1860 saw the end of this verbal sparring with the signing of a treaty, at first intended to be secret but whose contents were made public at the moment of ratification. To prove to the world the democratic justification of this land bargaining, plebiscites were held in April, first in Nice, then in Savoy. Both votes did indeed amply justify the political decisions that the two areas in question should become an integral part of metropolitan France. In Nice there were 25,743 voices 'for', with only 260 'against'; in Savoy 130,533 registered a 'yes', 235 a 'no', while 4,610 abstained.

Bibliography

Beales, Derek, *The Risorgimento and the unification of Italy*

Berkeley, G.F.M., *Italy in the making*

Bergot, Erwan, *The French Foreign Legion*

Brunon, Jean and Georges-R. Manue, *Le Livre d'or de la Légion Etrangère*

Bury, J.P.T., *Napoleon III and the Second Empire*

Cesarescu, E.M. Countess, *The Liberation of Italy, 1815-1870, Cavour*

Cobbin, Alfred, *A history of modern France from the 1st Empire to the 2nd Empire*

Crankshaw, Edward, *The fall of the house of Hapsburg*

Castelot, André, *Napoléon Trois*

Delzell, C.F., *The unification of Italy*

Dunant, Henri, *Un souvenir de Solferino*

Fleury, General Count, *Souvenirs*

Forester, C., *The life of Victor Emmanuel II*

Guedalla, P., *The Second Empire*

Garibaldi, Giuseppe, *Memoirs (edited by A. Duman)*

Guerzani, *Garibaldi*

Griffith, G.O., *Mazzini; prophet of modern Europe*

Hales, E.E.Y., *Mazzini and the secret societies*

Holt, Edgar, *Risorgimento – the making of Italy*

Italian General Staff, *Official history of the 1859 campaign, L'armata Sada a San Martino La insurrezione milanese de marzo 1848*

Janatschek, Ottaka, *The Emperor Franz Josef*

Lamb, Richard, *Novara*

Mack Smith, *The making of Italy, Victor Emmanuel, Cavour, and the risorgimento*

Macartney, C.A., *The Hapsburg Empire*
Mazziotti, *Napoleon III and Italy*
Orsi, Pietro, *Cavour and the making of modern Italy*
Packe, M.S.J., *The bombs of Orsini*
Russell, Odo., *The Roman question (extracts from despatches)*
Shed, Alan, *Radetsky; the imperial army*
Turnbull, Patrick, *Eugénie of the French*
War diaries, *2nd Foreign Legion infantry regiment*
Whyte, A.J., *Political life and letters of Cavour*
Zédé, General, *Souvenirs*

(The Bodleian Library, Oxford holds copies of many Italian
    Government publications, a large number dealing with
    the Risorgimento)

Index